ARTHUR MILLER, DRAMATIST

ARTHUR MILLER, DRAMATIST

EDWARD MURRAY

FREDERICK UNGAR PUBLISHING CO.
NEW YORK

Excerpts from copyrighted material as noted below
have been included with the kind permission
of the following publishers:

Oxford University Press, Inc.
White Collar: The American Middle Class,
by C. Wright Mills, 1951

Simon and Schuster, Inc.
The Art of Dramatic Writing, by Lajos Egri,
copyright 1946 by Lajos Egri

The Viking Press, Inc.
Collected Plays of Arthur Miller

Second Printing, 1967

For my wife, Peg

PREFACE

There would seem to be little need to justify a book on Arthur Miller. In spite of his continuing international reputation, Miller's plays have not yet received the close analytical study they demand. Generally his work has been extravagantly praised or viciously attacked without benefit of supporting evidence from the text. Critics, in fact, have been mainly concerned with whether or not *Death of a Salesman,* say, is in the tradition of "true" tragedy and with the autobiographical content, political and sexual, in his work. Although a play is obviously a totality, fragmentation is the shortcoming, to express it charitably, of all Miller criticism up to the present.

This study, then, focuses wholly on Miller's major plays, from *All My Sons* (1947), the first work that Miller himself felt was worthy of inclusion in his *Collected Plays,* to *Incident at Vichy* (1965), and, in order to have sufficient space to deal extensively with them, ignores such crude early efforts as the one-act *That They May Win* (1943) and the three-act *The Man Who Had All the Luck* (1944). The interested reader will also have to seek elsewhere for a discussion of Miller's novel *Focus* (1945), his adaptation of Ibsen's *An Enemy of the People* (1950), his radio plays, and his various commercial short stories. My method is rigorously inductive. Each play is approached as a unique entity, and *all* the parts—structure, character, dialogue, and theme—are studied.

It might be objected that I have not given adequate attention to Miller's language *as* language. Admittedly, Miller's language is, in itself, far from "poetic" (it need hardly be stressed, however, that Miller is not alone among distinguished modern dramatists in this respect), and a study that labored on this feature of his art would merely report the obvious in play after play. But there is another way to view dialogue, namely, in terms of its ability to forward the action, to reveal character, and to extend the thematic scope of the action, and in my analyses of the plays I have not neglected this side of Miller's art but have seen it in relation to structure, character and theme. Some readers might also feel that I have devoted too much space to a summary of the action in each play. My rationale for this neutral account of progression, however, is that too often Miller's critics, sometimes through carelessness, have failed to describe these simple facts correctly. Therefore, especially detailed explications of *Death of a Salesman* and *A View from the Bridge* are given in an effort to determine whether, as influential and persistent claims have it, these plays are "split" structurally and thematically.

E.M.

EDITIONS CITED

Collected Plays. New York: Viking, 1957 (includes *All My Sons, Death of a Salesman, The Crucible, A Memory of Two Mondays* and *A View from the Bridge*).

A View from the Bridge: Two One-Act Plays. New York: Viking, 1955 (contains the original version of *A View from the Bridge*).

The Misfits. New York: Viking, 1961.

After the Fall. New York: Viking, 1964.

Incident at Vichy. New York: Viking, 1965.

A bibliography of criticism on Miller arranged by chapter and play appears at the end of the book.

CONTENTS

CHAPTER ONE

All My Sons

All My Sons (1947), which earned Miller the Drama Critics Circle Award for the season, is a tightly constructed three-act play. In his "Introduction" to the Collected Plays, Miller has explained his purposes in the following manner:

> The form of All My Sons is a reflection and expression of several forces. . . . I desired above all to write rationally. . . . If there is one word to name the mood I felt it was Forego. Let nothing interfere with the shape, the direction, the intention. . . . My intention . . . was to be as untheatrical as possible. To that end any metaphor, any image, any figure of speech, however creditable to me, was removed if it even slightly brought to consciousness the hand of a writer. So far as was possible nothing was to be permitted to interfere with its artlessness. . . . I wanted then to write so that people of common sense would mistake my play for life itself and not be required to lend it some poetic license before it could be believed. I wanted to make the moral world as real and evident as the immoral one so splendidly is. (pp. 15-19)

The time-sequence in All My Sons covers less than twenty-four hours: Act One opens "early Sunday morning"; Act Two begins "that evening"; and Act Three commences at "Two o'clock the following morning." There is a single setting: the backyard of the Keller family "in the outskirts of an American town." Action proceeds along a single line, culminating in a climactic explosion.

In Act One, Miller is at pains to set the stage carefully for the action which follows. Thus, about the first half of the opening act is merely introductory in nature. Miller's strategy here is to focus steadily on Joe Keller as a prosperous businessman, devoted husband and father, and friendly neighbor. As Joe reclines in his yard, scanning the Sunday papers and talking to his neighbors, he emerges as a simple but shrewd man of middle age, whose eldest son, Larry, was reported missing during the Second World War, and whose wife, Kate, influenced by a neighbor's horoscope, refuses to believe that Larry is dead. The younger son, Chris, who returned safely from the war has invited Ann, Larry's old girlfriend, to visit the Kellers. When Chris informs Joe that he plans to marry Ann, Joe warns his son that if he does so it will destroy Kate's dream that Larry will one day return. Conflict is focused sharply when Chris threatens to take Ann to New York. This upsets Joe because the move will be a rejection of the Keller business, and the business means everything to Joe. Each of the three chief characters, then—Joe, Kate, and Chris—is seen to have something vital at stake. In the introduction various suggestions are made about a guilty secret in Joe's past, but the problem becomes more than a vague hint when Kate objects to a game that Joe is playing with a neighbor's boy, a game that Kate calls a "jail business" one, and Joe, "alarmed" and "angered," asks: "What have I got to hide?" To this Kate replies: "I didn't say you had anything to hide. . . ." (p. 74). This is the point of attack, which occurs slightly past the middle of Act One, for, although conflict is foreshadowed earlier, the major dramatic question—Joe's probable guilt—is unmistakably pointed to here for the first time. Miller has said:

Its first act was later called slow, but it was designed to be slow. It was made so that even boredom might

threaten, so that when the first intimation of the crime
is dropped a genuine horror might begin to move into the
heart of the audience . . . born of the contrast between
the placidity of the civilization on view and the threat to
it that a rage of conscience could create. ("Introduction,"
p. 18)

This problem will be discussed below in my criticism of the
structure.

In the last half of Act One, Ann appears and informs Kate
that she has stopped waiting for Larry to return. Kate, however,
remains inflexible in her belief. Exposition reveals that Joe and
Ann's father had both been in jail for shipping defective airplane parts during the war, an action which resulted in the death
of twenty-one American pilots, but that Joe had managed to get
exonerated by claiming to be ill at home the day that the parts
were shipped. Ann's father, however, remained in prison. Chris
and Ann, who consider Ann's father a murderer, cannot understand Joe's tolerant attitude toward his former partner. Chris is
especially critical on the subject because his conscience troubles
him about his returning alive from the war when so many of his
company died in combat. Ann assures Chris, however, that he
has a right to happiness. The curtain descends on an ominous
note with the report that George, Ann's brother, after visiting
his father in jail, is coming to visit the Kellers.

Conflict rises in Act Two when George accuses Joe of being
guilty of the crime which has ruined George's family. The
Kellers manage to placate George, and for a little while the situation seems more promising for the Kellers. It is Kate, finally,
who destroys the pretense of Joe's innocence when she blunders
and says: "[Joe] hasn't been laid up in fifteen years" (p. 111).
This "slip of the tongue" reveals the deception that Joe has
perpetrated, and from this revelation—which is the turning
point of the play—various effects swiftly result. George demands
that Ann leave the house with him, and Kate, for her own rea-

sons, agrees with George. When Chris refuses to part from Ann,
Kate says:

> Your brother's alive, darling, because if he's dead, your
> father killed him . . . God does not let a son be killed by
> his father. Now you see, don't you? (p. 114)

Chris then confronts Joe with the dramatic question suggested
in Act One at the point of attack: "Then . . . you did it?"
(p. 114). Presently Joe confesses, and the curtain falls on a confused Chris: "What must I do . . . what must I do?" (p. 116).
   In Act Three, Joe tells Kate: "If there's something bigger
than [the family] I'll put a bullet in my head!" (p. 120). This
line is preparation for Joe's suicide six and a half pages later.
According to Joe, Larry was not like Chris; Larry was "practical": "To him the world had a forty-foot front, it ended at the
building line" (p. 121). Ann enters, announces that she will not
expose Joe, but insists that Kate release Chris from feeling
"guilty with me" (p. 121). When Kate refuses, Ann declares
that Larry is dead. After sending Joe into the house, Ann produces a letter which was written by Larry on the day that he
died. Chris enters with Joe and it is related that Chris hesitates
to deliver Joe to justice because the business world shares the
guilt with Joe. After reading Larry's letter, however, Chris
changes his mind, for the letter reveals that Larry was not so
"practical" as Joe had supposed. This is the crisis of the play. In
the letter, Larry says:

> they flew in a load of papers from the States and I read
> about Dad and your father being convicted . . . I can't
> bear to live any more. . . . How could he have done that?
> Every day three or four men never come back and he sits
> back there doing business. . . . I'm going out on a mission
> in a few minutes. They'll probably report me missing. If

they do, I want you to know that you musn't wait for me. I tell you, Ann, . . . I could kill him— (p. 126)

The climax occurs when Joe offers to surrender himself to justice. Kate, however, argues with him: "Larry was your son . . . he'd never tell you to do this"; to which Joe replies: "I think to him they were all my sons. And I guess they were. . . ." (p. 126). While Joe is inside the house, Chris tells Kate:

Once and for all you can know there's a universe of people outside and you're responsible to it, and unless you know that, you threw away your son because that's why he died. (pp. 126-127)

Immediately "a shot is heard in the house" (p. 127). Joe has put a bullet in his head—for Larry has evidently shown Joe that there is "something bigger" than the "family." The play concludes with Chris "almost crying," but with Kate telling him: "Don't take it on yourself. . . . Live!" (p. 127).

Although the structure of *All My Sons* is tight, it remains open to a number of serious criticisms. My summary of the introduction in Act One focuses on essential items only and thus fails to reveal the repetition and inconsequential byplay contained in the first sixteen pages of the text. Miller would have it that every step in *All My Sons* was carefully calculated. We need not necessarily accept this view. The critic who wrote the "Introduction" in 1957 was not the dramatist who wrote the play in 1947. Granting, for the sake of argument, that every move in the play was carefully plotted, one might question whether contrast, which is indeed a powerful dramatic device, could not have been established in a more economical manner, whether a relatively static and lengthy introduction threatening "boredom" was absolutely essential. A more cautious approach might suggest that Miller, in his second full-length play, had not as yet thoroughly mastered certain difficult problems of craft—chiefly, as Miller himself acknowledges, "the biggest single dramatic problem, namely, how to dramatize what has gone before" ("Introduction," p. 21).

In addition, Miller seems guilty of having made his dramatic problem easy for himself at the turning point of the play. A "slip of the tongue" is certainly possible, but in the context of the play, is it not made to seem fortuitous? And is it not precisely the fortuitous nature of events that the form of the play is at pains to deny? According to Miller: "the structure of the play is designed to bring a man into the direct path of the consequences he has wrought" ("Introduction," p. 18); and: "The fortress which *All My Sons* lays siege to is the fortress of unrelatedness" ("Introduction," p. 19). How is Kate's "slip of the tongue" related to the events of the play? Not only by intention, but through the achieved tightness of structure, Miller forces the reader to question the logic of his play. The most influential interpretation of verbal "slips" in our time is, of course, the Freudian one. Miller, however, provides no evidence in the play for such an interpretation; in fact, there is no explanation given for Kate's "slip"—it must simply be attributed to chance. In dramatic terms, then, the "slip" is not made plausible. When one considers the events that immediately follow upon Kate's blunder, one is inclined to feel that Miller has not faced the dramatic task in a forthright manner.

The arbitrary nature of the action continues in Act Three. Aside from the crude foreshadowing device quoted in my summary, Joe Keller shows no evidence of being a potential suicide. As a description of his character will reveal shortly, Joe is lacking in inner conflict; but if modern psychology has taught us anything, it is that none of us—least of all a suicide—is lacking in inner conflict. Kate, it should be noted, is made to threaten suicide in Act One; she says: "if [Larry's] not coming back, then I'll kill myself!" (p. 73). This, like Joe's threat in Act Three, looks like foreshadowing. It is beside the point to say that it is in character for Kate to choose life over death. Perhaps, one might argue, Miller intends that Kate's refusal to kill herself reflects freedom in the world of his play; it demonstrates that Joe is not being jerked about arbitrarily by the author, that Joe wills his own destruction. Whatever the rationale behind the strategy, however, it seems to make for confusion rather than complexity, for it tends to weaken Joe's motivation instead of making it appear freely chosen. The question arises: Why *must* Joe kill himself? (One critic has speculated why Joe is strong enough to bear the guilt of his first act but not strong enough to shoulder the second guilt.) One is forced to conclude that Joe Keller kills himself because his suicide is an effective way to drive home the thesis.

The appearance of the letter in Act Three is the most censured device in the play. Only Dennis Welland defends it; he argues that the device is credible, economical, and dramatic. This is a valiant critical defense, but no more convincing, finally, than the play itself. As Kate brought about the turning point, Larry—a character never seen on stage—prepares the climax. The focus, it seems, should be on Joe, not Kate, or Larry, or even Chris. The audience should be made to see— should have been made to see from the first—the slow stages of Joe's movement toward self-destruction. This is why the leisurely introduction is blameworthy. Twenty-four hours is a short time in which to propel a man from "placidity" to a "rage of conscience." The letter itself might very well be "credible" and "economical"; this, however, is not enough. It is, for one thing, a stock device suggesting the "well-made play." Most critics, including the present one, are inclined to feel that the letter is not dramatically convincing. Contrivance also suggests itself in the stagy juxtaposition of Chris's indictment of his parents and the resounding report that immediately follows signalizing the end of Joe Keller's existence. This too is an "economical" and "dramatic" way to drive home the thesis.

The question has been raised about who the protagonist is,

structurally, in *All My Sons*. According to one critic, Miller never focuses clearly on Joe Keller; although Joe is central thematically, Chris appears to receive equal attention. According to a second critic, the interest shifts from the protagonist to the antagonist. Some facts are in order. Out of a total number of sixty-eight pages of text, Joe is present on about forty-five pages; Chris is present on about forty-nine pages. Out of a total number of sixty-two scenes, Joe appears in forty-four and Chris in forty-two. A check of speaking lines would reveal the same fairly equal distribution of parts between Joe and Chris. Quantitatively, then, there is a basis for asking who is the protagonist in *Sons*. Qualitatively, analysis seems to suggest that Chris, not Joe, is the most active character in the play. Until the final moments of the last act, Joe is relatively passive. Chris, however, forces the conflict from beginning to end. It is Chris who invites Ann to visit the Keller house; Chris who wants to remove the fiction of Larry's return; Chris who challenges Kate's obsession; Chris who calls Joe to defend his acts; Chris who demands that Joe atone for his crime against humanity. Although Joe carries the burden of the theme, then, Chris is the driving force within the structure. This dichotomy, I believe, damages the play. Not all plays, of course, have an active protagonist (which seems like a contradiction in terms); *Othello* springs quickly to mind. One hesitates to generalize here, for each play must be viewed on its own merits. In *All My Sons*, the shift in emphasis would seem unhappy because Joe's movement toward suicide should be made credible, and, if that movement is to be made credible, the focus should be almost wholly on Joe. It is not that some dramatic "law" demands that Joe seal his own fate. It is that by the logic of *this* play, *All My Sons*, that Joe Keller must convincingly advance to his final gesture as a dramatic character.

This raises, finally, several minor questions of probability. One critic has questioned the appearance of George in Act Two. George had not visited his father since the latter was sentenced to jail. Over three years had passed without George sending his father a Christmas card (p. 101). Why, then, did George suddenly visit his father? George tells Ann: "I wanted to . . . tell him you were going to be married. It seemed impossible not to tell him" (p. 101). One might also consider the engagement of Chris and Ann. When Joe asks "why it has to be Annie," Chris says: "Because it is" (p. 68). Joe, baffled, points out that it is "five years" since Chris has seen Ann, but Chris says:

> I can't help it. I know her best. I was brought up next door to her. These years when I think of someone for my wife, I think of Annie. What do you want, a diagram? (p. 68)

Ann admits that she almost "got married two years ago," but that Chris started writing to her then and she had "felt something"—in fact, she had "felt something" ever since. She did not write, however, because: "I was waiting for you, Chris. Till then you never wrote. And when you did, what did you say? You sure can be ambiguous, you know" (p. 84). The reader suspects that Chris's "ambiguity" stems from his author's desire to save Ann for a crucial moment in the lives of his other characters. There is, in short, too much contrivance here. Why, after ignoring his father for three years, did George suddenly find it "impossible" not to inform the man of Ann's approaching marriage? Why this sudden necessity for respect? One might feel that there is no adequate reason here—except that Miller simply wanted George for the second act. Similarly, the romance between Chris and Ann does not encourage close scrutiny. There is something vague, even a little "mystical," about the coming together of the two lovers that suggests love less than manipulation. These are minor matters, however, and need not be overemphasized—they merely underline more important structural defects.

Ironically Miller, who had intended to write a play that
would be "as untheatrical as possible," that would be distinguished by its "artlessness," actually produced the apotheosis
of the theatrical and the artful—in other words, a "well-made
play." And as William Archer says: "The trouble with the
well-made play is that it is almost always . . . ill-made."

Are the characters in *All My Sons* "ill-made," too? Miller,
in his opening stage directions, describes Joe Keller in this
manner:

> Keller is nearing sixty. A heavy man of stolid mind and
> build, a business man these many years, but with the im-
> print of the machine-shop worker and boss still upon
> him. When he reads, when he speaks, when he listens,
> it is with the terrible concentration of the uneducated
> man for whom there is wonder in many commonly
> known things, a man whose judgments must be dredged
> out of experience and a peasant-like common sense. A
> man among men. (pp. 58-59)

It has been said that there is more "social density" in *All My
Sons* than in Miller's previous play. One function of dialogue
is to reveal character; it should throw light on the character's
past, present, and future. If we examine *All My Sons*, do we
find language projecting a dense, complex social world—what,
specifically, do we learn about Joe Keller? In Act Three, Joe
says:

> I should've put [Chris] out when he was ten like I was
> put out, and make him earn his keep. Then he'd know
> how a buck is made in this world. (p. 120)

This, plus other remarks in the play, indicates that Joe went
to work at an early age, that he worked hard, that he had no

education, that society in the past fifty years has grown increasingly specialized and complex, and that Joe is somewhat baffled by the changes. Joe is a product of a business society; his ideal is General Motors (p. 109). Joe's every move, even to shipping defective airplane parts, seems inspired by business values:

> I'm in business . . . a hundred and twenty cracked, you're out of business . . . they close you up . . . you lay forty years into a business and they knock you out in five minutes, what could I do, let them take forty years, let them take my life away? (p. 115)

Joe can be cynical about the "big ones": "a little man makes a mistake and they hang him by the thumbs; the big ones become ambassadors" (p. 109). He can, however, also grow vehement:

> Did they ship a gun or a truck outa Detroit before they got their price? Is that clean? It's dollars and cents, nickles and dimes; war and peace . . . what's clean? (p. 125)

This completes Joe's social dimension.

Psychologically, Joe is depicted as a humble man; he repeatedly scores his own ignorance (p. 60). His sense of humor is described by Chris: "George Bernard Shaw as an elephant" (p. 86). Joe knows how to be "practical" in a ruthless society: "I ignore," says Joe, "what I gotta ignore" (p. 68). He boasts about his "guts" in braving the neighbors after his trial (pp. 80-81). He seems open and straightforward, but he is capable of deceit and deception; he says: "I never believed in crucifying people" (p. 81)—when he has, in fact crucified his best friend, Ann's father. And, finally, Joe is a "family man":

> There's nothin' [Chris] could do that I wouldn't forgive. Because he's my son. Because I'm his father and he's my son. (p. 120)

This is Miller's description of Chris:

> He is thirty-two; like his father, solidly built, a listener. A man capable of immense affection and loyalty. (p. 64)

Does dialogue reveal much about Chris's background and social attitudes? Chris says that the "business doesn't inspire me" (p. 69); he explains:

> I like it an hour a day. If I have to grub for money all day long at least at evening I want it beautiful. I want a family, I want some kids, I want to build something I can give myself to. (p. 69)

Before the first act is over, however, Chris tells Ann: "I'm going to make a fortune for you!" (p. 86). According to Chris, America is a "zoo" (p. 124). In combat, however, it was, says Chris, different:

> They didn't die; they killed themselves for each other. . . . And I got an idea—watching them go down. . . . A kind of—responsibility. Man for man. . . . And then I came home and it was incredible . . . the whole thing to them was a kind of a—bus accident. I went to work with Dad, and that ratrace again. (p. 85)

Psychologically, Chris has many traits. Jim says that Chris "likes everybody" (p. 75). Chris shows that he is not Christ, however, for he cannot forgive everything, he cannot forgive what he regards as unforgivable, namely, the crime that has sent Ann's father to prison (p. 81). Nevertheless, Chris is long-suffering: "every time I reach out for something I want," he says, "I have to pull back because other people will suffer" (p. 68). Yet Chris is determined to find happiness. He admits to being "old-fashioned"—he "loves his parents" (p. 83). When evidence of Joe's guilt is manifest, however, Chris finally demands that his parent be punished. Chris has "no imagination" (p. 84); he admits to being "ignorant" (p. 64). He also confesses to being "not fast with women" (p. 68). As has been said, Chris has a sense of guilt; the war, he says: "seemed to make suckers out of a lot of guys. I felt wrong to be alive, to open the bank-book, to drive the new car" (p. 85). The dialogue of other characters casts additional light on Chris. Says Joe: "everything bothers [Chris]. You make a deal, overcharge two cents, and his hair falls out" (p. 121). Sue, a neighbor, says: "if Chris wants people to put on the hairshirt let him take off his broadcloth" (p. 94). Says Jim, Sue's husband: "I always had the feeling that in the back of his head, Chris . . . almost knew [about Joe]"—but Jim adds: "Chris would never know how to live with a thing like that. It takes a certain talent—for lying" (p. 118). Chris himself says: "I'm yellow . . . because I suspected my father and I did nothing. . . ." (p. 123).

In his stage directions, Miller says that Kate "is in her early fifties, a woman of uncontrolled inspirations and an overwhelming capacity for love" (p. 69). In the play itself, Kate criticizes Larry, Chris, and George: "You had big principles, Eagle Scouts the three of you. . . ." (p. 107). George, who lost his girl, Lydia, to a 4F, Frank, is told: "While you were getting mad about Fascism Frank was getting into [Lydia's] bed" (p. 107). The ultimate wisdom is: "look after yourself" (p. 108). Kate cares little if Chris's "idealism" dies—the important thing is that he return to the family (p. 118). When Kate meets George, Miller says: "her pity, open and unabashed, reaches into him" (p. 104); and Kate says: "it breaks my heart to see what happened to all the children" (p. 105). Kate calls herself

"stupid" (p. 90). Perhaps that is why she is scornful of intel-
lect, for she informs Chris and George that they "*think* too
much" (p. 106). Kate tells Ann: "Listen to your heart. Only
your heart" (p. 78). Kate is also fond of omens: "[Ann] goes to
sleep in [Larry's] room," she says, "and his memorial breaks in
pieces" (p. 73). Trusting in Frank's star-book, she can say:

> certain things have to be, and certain things can never
> be. . . . That's why there's God. Otherwise anything
> could happen. But there's God, so certain things can
> never happen. (p. 78)

Perhaps the most trenchant remark concerning Kate is made by
Jim, when he says that Kate has "a certain talent—for lying"
(p. 118). Her final word—"Live" (p. 127)—is in character, for
Kate has revealed her ability to put unpleasant facts out of
mind and "live" all through the play; in this, lies Kate Keller's
strength . . . and her weakness.

Physically, none of Miller's characters is individualized in a
striking way. Perhaps this is not a serious failing, however, in
a form where there are actors to impersonate the playwright's
creations. Certainly the stage directions characterize Joe sharply
enough, and, as pointed out earlier, Miller reveals in action (to
the point of "boredom"?) the features of Joe described in the
directions. Although certain facts are related about Joe's background and social attitudes through dialogue, much else is also
left blank. We learn nothing about Joe's parents, nothing
about his childhood thoughts and feelings (a time, according
to moralists and psychologists, when one's character is more
or less molded for life), nothing about where Joe came from,
nothing, save "the outskirts of an American town," about where
he is at present. For a "realistic" play, the dialogue, then, is
not wholly satisfactory. Psychologically, Joe has a number of
traits; he is not presented under a single aspect. Nevertheless,
he remains unsuitable for his specific role. More than an ac-

cumulation of traits are required here—the need is for contra-
dictory traits that will directly influence the course of action.
Joe Keller lacks these traits.

Dialogue similarly fails to reveal much, if anything, about
Chris's childhood, boyhood, or young manhood. We learn only
that Ann's family were neighbors to the Kellers while the children were growing. Chris, however, remains a more complex
character than Joe. Chris, for example, is in conflict between
the "love ethic" (p. 69) and the "business ethic" (p. 86), but
Joe, presumably, feels no such conflict. Chris is also torn between loyalty to Ann and loyalty to his mother; between suspicion of Joe and the need to conceal his doubts from himself.
If Joe is easier to believe in than his idealistic son, it is because
Joe's philosophy seems to rise up palpably from the concrete
and visible action on stage; but Chris must reach back to the
past for an actualization of his philosophy (as Miller must
reach back into the past for an unseen character to untie the
knot). What we get is a *summary* of Chris's development (p.
85) rather than a *dramatic experience* of the thing itself. Consequently, Chris's "ideals" risk sounding too abstract—particularly when Chris, like Joe, yearns for family life and fortune,
too. The fact that dialogue fails to illuminate Chris's background likewise militates against our belief in his values. Perhaps Miller is counting on a stock response here. Why should
Chris differ from Joe and Kate? What specific factors account
for the difference? The war experience does not seem entirely
satisfactory as an explanation. Not all the fighting men were
so "responsible"; not all the civilians regarded the war as a "bus
accident." There is a danger of sentimentality here, the tendency to dichotomize humanity into "good guys" and "bad
guys"—in short, a melodramatic vision. Lacking social depth,
then, Chris often seems to step out of character to deliver a
speech (pp. 126-127). Like other aspects of the play, the language is frequently too "neat," too obviously didactic.

At first sight, Kate Keller seems complex. A closer view,

however, suggests that there is perhaps confusion interlaced with complexity in her characterization. It is Miller's attitude, as reflected in his stage directions, that are disconcerting. Miller says Kate has "uncontrolled inspirations"—but after threatening to kill herself, Kate manages to control her "inspiration." Miller says that Kate has an "overwhelming capacity for love" —but the play shows that her love has strict limits; like Joe's love, it has a "forty-foot front." Miller says that Kate feels pity for George—but the play shows that Kate, as much as Joe, destroyed George's family. This is not a problem in the theater; for an audience, Kate is a self-deceived woman; but for a reader, there is something incongruous in Miller's conception of Kate. Not satisfactory for either audience or reader, however, is the fact that Kate's dialogue fails to reveal anything at all about her background or development.

Only Chris really grows in the play. Joe is made to grow— and his "jump" is unconvincing. Kate is static. She has experienced some unpleasant events, but there is no indication that she has altered any of her basic attitudes. In Act One, Chris feels guilty and vaguely suspects Joe; in Act Two, he learns the truth about Joe, but cannot immediately demand Joe's expiation—hence, his sense of guilt *increases*; but in Act Three, Larry's suicide reveals the course that Chris must take, and when the play ends, Chris is presumably free from his sense of guilt and able to enjoy life again. Although the letter device tends to weaken Chris's development too, his movement as a whole seems relatively steady and credible. There has also been preparation for his final action.

None of the minor characters requires detailed discussion. All of them are "flat"; all of them are static. A few of them, such as Bert, Lydia, and Frank, seem superfluous in terms of action. Whether all of them are necessary to the development of the theme will be taken up below. Contrast is not very diverse here; Joe, Kate, Sue, and, to a lesser degree, Frank, are played off against Chris, Ann, George, and Jim. The contrast is a simple one—between those who have "ideals" and those who have no "ideals," or, at least, very limited ones. The minor characters are stock figures: Jim is the "country doctor"; Sue is the "shrew"; George is the "avenger." Frank, unlike the other minor figures, has an interesting psychology, but if you hold that a play should have no spare parts, a case could be made for Frank being unnecessary. Lydia and Bert have no discernible substance. Ann, of course, is the most disappointing character among the minor roles simply because of her position in the plot. A close reading of the text will yield next to nothing about Ann's background, traits, or social attitude. But perhaps these characters can be discussed with more profit in relation to the theme of the play.

In his "Introduction," Miller says:

> In its earlier versions the mother . . . was in a dominating position . . . her astrological beliefs were given great prominence . . . because I sought in every sphere to give body and life to connection. But as the play progressed the conflict between Joe and . . . Chris pressed astrology to the wall until its mysticism gave way to psychology. There was also the impulse to regard the mystical with suspicion, since it had, in the past, given me only turgid works that could never develop a true climax based upon revealed psychological truths. . . . [Kate's] obsession now had to be opened up to reveal its core of self-interest. . . . ("Introduction," p. 20)

The key speech of Kate appears near the end of Act Two (p. 114, quoted above). Here, the "astrological" and the "psychological" meet. Whereas Joe blames the "system," Kate shifts responsibility to "God." The action of the play, however, denies that responsibility can be shifted in this fashion. Kate's "core of self-interest" is also revealed—she believes what she wants to believe. It was noted earlier that for Kate the "heart," not the "head," is the trustworthy part of the anatomy. The play itself, once more, affirms the opposite belief. Chris listens to his "heart" when he hesitates to deliver Joe to justice, but Larry uses his "head," his suicide being a vote for "responsibility" beyond blood ties. Joe and Kate have not been able to identify Larry and Chris with other young men. We are given to understand that Larry never flew a P40; when Joe states this as a fact, nobody contradicts him (p. 114). When Ann asks: "how do you know Larry wasn't one of them?" (Ann knows the truth, of course, but she is trying to make a point here, namely, that the Kellers should not morally dissociate the crime from Larry's death), Kate replies: "As long as you're here, Annie, I want to ask you never to say that again" (p. 81). This line looks forward to Kate's key speech already quoted. There is a problem here, however, that will be analyzed in a moment.

Do the minor characters have significant thematic relevance? Sue says: "Chris makes people want to be better than it's possible to be" (p. 93), which remark links up with Joe's statement: "Chris, a man can't be Jesus in this world!" (p. 125). The play "refutes" both. Frank ("that big dope," as Kate puts it, "who never reads anything but Andy Gump. . . ." [p. 108]) would seem to lie somewhere between the two contrasting camps mentioned previously. George says: "When I was studying [law] in the hospital it seemed sensible, but outside there doesn't seem to be much of a law" (p. 100). Jim says: "I can't find myself; it's even hard sometimes to remember the kind of man I wanted to be" (p. 118). Ann's commitment is clear from the fact that her "ideals" prevent her from forgiving her father for his crime (p. 81).

A close study of the crisis and climax of Act Three shows clearly that Joe is not, as one critic has asserted, exonerated; otherwise, why does Miller laboriously introduce the letter and why does Joe, as a consequence, destroy himself? No, one does not necessarily accuse Miller of intellectual confusion here; it is Joe who rationalizes and Chris who, for a time, hesitates and seems to accept the rationalization. Nevertheless, one feels that, in spite of the ending, Miller is also blaming the system. Miller does not seem to say, though, that the system determines man (how could he, in view of the ending?); he suggests, rather, that the system has a strong influence on man. Is this, in the light of sociological data, an unreasonable attitude? Psychologically, it is entirely credible that a son might hesitate for a time to send his own father to prison. (Whether knowingly to withhold shipments of war supplies until a price is fixed, while the lives of fighting men depend on those supplies, is *morally* poles apart from what Joe perpetrated remains a nice point for an ethical philosopher or moral theologian to ponder.) Miller might be open to the charge of not sufficiently distinguishing moral from legal guilt, but in view of what has been said, it would be difficult to make the charge hold—considering the situation of the characters and the ending of the play.

In the discussion of character it was suggested that Kate seemed somewhat confusing as a creation, at least as she appears in the stage directions. It is possible that in the course of his numerous revisions of the play, Miller lost his clear focus on Kate. The question arises, why would Kate connect Joe's crime with Larry's death (and we must believe that Kate knows that Larry never flew a P40) if she had not, from the start, made the logical transition from "my son, Larry" to . . . "why, they are all my sons"? Joe made this transition ("jump") only when faced with the fact of Larry's suicide—but how did Kate arrive at this state of consciousness? Whatever one's own epistemology, within the context of the play—that is, in the projected polar opposites of "heart" and "head"—it is the "heart" that is suspect, the "head" that is noble. Kate's "heart," then, appears to arrive at a truth that presumably only the "head" can know. Kate is at the core of the plot; her refusal to relinquish her obsession is a source of conflict in the play; her "slip of the tongue" brings about the turning point in the action; and her inflexibility drives Ann into revealing Larry's letter, thus forcing the play to its climax and conclusion. Thematically, however, Kate adds nothing to Joe's characterization, nothing to the basic thrust of the play—in fact, as has been suggested, Kate tends to confuse rather than project the theme.

None of the minor characters seems absolutely essential to the theme. Frank, for example, appears unnecessary because whatever he might contribute to the meaning of the play is already inherent in Kate's role—one stargazer would seem sufficient. It might also be noted that the use of the stars is a crude way to focus the theme; it too overtly suggests "fate in the stars." Equally unfortunate is the too obvious play on Chris as "Christ." Only Ann and George are really integrated with the action. The others are there, no doubt, because Miller felt that their presence added complexity and social extension to the play. They add, in fact, no complexity. Structurally, they delay the point of attack, and that delay has repercussions on the credibility of Joe's development. Thematically, it is questionable whether they succeed in making the play more "significant." Where would one draw the line here? Is the formula: the more characters, the more extension and significance? It would not seem to be a mere matter of numbers. Economy demands that no character is strictly necessary who does not contribute something vital to action or theme. A more liberal view would leave room for a certain amount of "excess baggage" here—but Miller, it seems, has been rather too liberal on this score. In *Ghosts* (a play that many consider Ibsen's masterpiece), there are only five characters—half the number of *All My Sons*—yet Ibsen manages to project a complex social vision.

It has been asserted that *All My Sons* is actually a vote for the family instead of loyalty to the state ("something bigger" than the "family"), for, so the argument goes, Miller does not make clear whether the soldiers under Chris were devoted to an abstract ideal or merely attached to the group—if the latter, it is simply the family in disguise. Although Miller tends to idealize the American soldier, the abstract ideal in the play *is* precisely loyalty to one another, which might be described as a "family" loyalty, but obviously the "family" here extends beyond the narrow limits of one's immediate blood ties. It is an incomplete "family" loyalty only in the sense that it does not include the enemy.

I have suggested that *All My Sons* is a thesis play. Miller says: "I think now that the straight-forwardness of the . . . form was in some part due to the relatively sharp definition of the social aspects of the problem it dealt with" ("Introduction," p. 22). That the play is more complex than most critics, perhaps even including Miller, have allowed is certainly true. Whether it is complex enough, however, to weather the charge of thesis drama is another matter. Although Joe Keller and the other characters are not depicted as merely pawns of social forces, they *are* pawns of theatrical contrivance, a point which has been sufficiently discussed above. As for the "idea" itself, it would appear to be too explicitly insisted upon, too sermonic in deliverance, and, because sermons tend to oversimplify experience (even the laudable Sermon on the Mount has required volumes of exegesis), Miller seems guilty of ignoring the complexity of experience and the intractability of the human animal.

CHAPTER TWO

Death of a Salesman

Death of a Salesman: Certain Private Conversations in Two Acts and a Requiem (1949), Miller's second successful full-length play, greatly exceeds *All My Sons* in complexity of organization. In fact, its many alternations of time-sequence and its frequent shifts in point of view make summarizing the plot difficult. The following brief and bald description focuses solely on the most important facts and the main movement of the action, and it is only an introduction to the more detailed explication below.

When the play opens, Willy Loman, an aging and relatively unsuccessful traveling salesman, is on the verge of suicide. After more than thirty years (Willy says, "I put thirty-four years into this firm" [p. 181], but his wife says "thirty-six" [p. 163]), Willy's boss has reduced him to straight commission and Willy is forced to borrow money from his neighbor Charley in order to deceive Linda, his wife, about his inability to support her. Biff, Willy's beloved son, is, at thirty-five, a drifter and petty thief who has not fulfilled the promise of his early years when he was a high school football star. In Act One, Biff has returned from his wanderings to visit his parents, and he is joined by Happy, Willy's younger son, who is a minor functionary in a department store. Willy is bitterly disappointed in Biff, and Biff is hostile toward Willy. Willy's frustrated "success dream"—he has insisted that "appearances" and being "well liked" are keys to social advancement—is complicated by the fact that years ago Biff discovered Willy in a hotel with a strange woman. Since that time, Willy has been a "fake" to his son and an excuse for Biff's own failures. In the course of the play, Howard, Willy's boss, fires Willy; and Biff fails to secure a loan from a former employer who he had hoped would finance him in a business venture. In a cafe scene, Biff and Happy abandon their father and go off with two girls. At the climax of the play, however, Biff stops his "spiteful" behavior toward Willy and assumes responsibility for his life. Willy, moved by Biff's expression of love, kills himself in an effort to provide Biff a fresh start in life with his twenty-thousand dollar insurance policy. In the epilogue, Happy says that Willy had a "good dream . . . to come out number-one man." Biff, however, asserts that Willy had the "wrong dream."

Setting is an important element in *Death of a Salesman*. Miller's first two plays were presented in a rather bleak, naturalistic, "straight-forward" style. Miller himself has said that *All My Sons* "was not sensuous enough," adding that in *Salesman* he "wished to create a form which, in itself as a form, would literally be the process of Willy Loman's way of mind" ("Introduction," pp. 23-24). Setting provides a flexible medium in which to enact "the process of Willy Loman's way of mind." As will become apparent, setting contributes to the mood of the play. The main action takes place in and around Willy's house in Brooklyn, New York. A "solid vault of apartment houses," says Miller, surrounds Willy's "small, fragile-seeming home" (p. 130). Symbolism is also apparent in the following stage directions:

> An air of the dream clings to the place, a dream rising out of reality. The kitchen at center seems actual enough, for there is a kitchen table with three chairs, and a refrigerator. But no other fixtures are seen. (p. 130)

But setting is also "functional":

> The entire setting is wholly or, in some places, partially
> transparent. The roof-line of the house is one-dimen-
> sional; under and over it we see the apartment buildings.
> Before the house lies an apron, curving beyond the fore-
> stage into the orchestra. This forward area serves as the
> back yard as well as the locale of all Willy's imaginings
> and of his city scenes. Whenever the action is in the
> present the actors observe the imaginary wall-lines, enter-
> ing the house only through its door . . . but in the scenes
> of the past these boundaries are broken, and characters
> enter to leave a room by stepping "through" a wall onto
> the forestage (pp. 130-131).

In Act One, the time is somewhere between midnight and
dawn. In Act Two, it is the following morning. The last lines
of Act Two, and the Requiem that follows, move from the
night of the preceding day to another "day"—it could be the
following day or several days later. The action covers, then,
in "present," forward-moving time, about twenty-four hours.

Actually, time in *Salesman* is much more complex in treatment than the above summary suggests. In the play, three time-
sequences may be distinguished: first, there is "present" time,
that is, action moves forward in the present without reference
to the "return of the repressed" in Willy's mind—point of
view is wholly objective; secondly, there is "past" time, that is,
although the action remains in the present (this is not a flashback), we are wholly inside Willy's mind, viewing his imaginative reconstruction of the past—the point of view is wholly
subjective; thirdly, there is (for want of a better word) "simul-
tancity"; that is, the action remains in the present, but we are
not wholly inside Willy's mind, for there is both objective
reference to other characters and subjective projection by Willy
—point of view is objective-subjective.

Since alternation of the time-sequence and shift in point of
view is the most important structural element in *Salesman*, it

is the key to the action. As will be seen in a moment, movement results from progressive causal logic in the "present" interwoven with the mental reconstruction by Willy of his "past." It is the juxtaposing, and in some instances fusing, of these two patterns that constitutes dramatic structure in Miller's play. Hence, it would seem profitable to view the structure of *Salesman* in terms of its time-sequences (there are twenty-four such time-sequences). A brief consideration of each sequence, with the focus on exposition and foreshadowing, should reveal how Miller has attempted to complicate his action and has attempted to integrate structure around key scenes, each of which is designed to build toward the final climax of the play. This analysis, necessarily somewhat tedious, is perhaps the only way to establish a solid basis for resolving the many critical problems that have been raised by Miller's play.

ACT ONE

FIRST TIME-SEQUENCE. "Present" time. Place: Willy's house. It is the middle of the night and Willy has returned unexpectedly from a selling trip. He is exhausted. Willy confesses to Linda that he was afraid of driving off the road. (Preparation for Willy's suicide.) Willy says that old man Wagner—Willy's first boss—appreciated him, but Howard, Wagner's son, does not. Linda, however, convinces Willy that he must ask Howard for a job in New York. (Preparation for the scene in Howard's office.) Willy says a man spends a lifetime paying for a house— and then there is nobody to live in it. (Preparation for Linda's echo of this in the Requiem.) Willy is alternately angry at Biff for being "lost" and confident that Biff will yet be "big." (Preparation for the father-son conflict which is the core of the play. Thus, by the third page of dialogue, the point of attack has been completed, for Willy Loman has reached a turning point in his life, conflict has been foreshadowed, and the major

dramatic questions have been projected or suggested.) Willy
then becomes lost in memories of the past. (Preparation for the
shift in point of view.) Light fades on Willy and comes up on
Biff and Happy, upstairs. Happy asks Biff if he is "still sour" on
Willy and Biff replies: "He's all right, I guess." (Preparation
for Biff's ambivalence toward Willy.) Biff and Happy discuss
past sexual conquests. (Preparation for the cafe scene.) Happy
says that Willy talks to himself—and most of the time it is
about Biff. (More specific preparation for the shift in point of
view.) Biff, however, refused to take the blame for Willy's
problems. (Preparation for the hotel scene.) Nevertheless,
Biff decides to ask Bill Oliver, his old boss, for a loan—but
he trusts Oliver does not still think that Biff stole a carton of
basketballs from the store. (Preparation for Biff's confession in
the cafe scene.) Happy admits to not being content with his
job, but nonetheless declares that it is what he wants in life.
(Preparation for Happy's speech in the Requiem.) Willy is
then heard mumbling below. (Preparation for change in point
of view.) Biff is angry because Linda, he thinks, can hear
Willy. (Preparation for the hotel scene, for Biff believes that
Willy has a guilty conscience.) Light fades on the sons, and rises
on Willy. (pp. 131-142)

SECOND TIME-SEQUENCE. "Subjective" time. Place: Willy's
house as he re-creates his "past." Biff, about eighteen, shows
Willy a football he "borrowed" from school. Willy says the
coach will probably praise Biff for his "initiative." (Preparation
for the cafe scene and also the climax.) Willy vows that one
day he will be "bigger" than Charley because the latter is "not
well liked." (Preparation for Willy's later borrowing money
from Charley.) Willy promises to take Biff to New England
in the summer. (Preparation for the hotel scene.) Bernard,
Charley's boy, enters and says Biff will fail math if he doesn't
study. (Preparation for the hotel scene.) Willy says that Bernard might get good grades in school, but in the outside world
the Lomans will succeed because they have "appearance" and

are "well liked." (Preparation for the scene in Charley's office where Bernard, as a man, is a successful lawyer and Willy borrows money from Charley.) Willy brags to Linda about his big sales—but then ruefully admits to a low gross. (Preparation for Willy's ultimate "failure.") The Woman appears, laughing. (Preparation for the hotel scene.) Willy argues with Linda about Biff's waywardness. (Preparation for Biff's ultimate "failure.") Light fades. (pp. 142-151)

THIRD TIME-SEQUENCE. Place: Willy's house in the "present." Willy tells Happy that Ben—Willy's elder brother, now dead—had the right idea: he went to Alaska and became rich. (Preparation for Ben's appearance.) Charley enters and offers Willy a job, but Willy refuses. (Contrasts with the previous time-sequence.) (pp. 152-154)

FOURTH TIME-SEQUENCE. Time: "simultaneity." While Willy and Charley play cards, Ben appears, and while Willy speaks in the "present" to Charley, he re-creates the "past" with Ben. Finally, Charley exits. (pp. 154-156)

FIFTH TIME-SEQUENCE. Time: "past." Ben is critical of Willy's job, but Willy tries to convince Ben that there is a future in selling. (Preparation for the scene in Howard's office.) Charley enters and criticizes Willy for permitting his sons to steal. Ben seems to approve of the boys' "fearlessness." (Preparation for the decline of Ben's brand of "individualism" and the day when everything, as Willy puts it, is "cut and dried.") (pp. 156-160)

SIXTH TIME-SEQUENCE. Place: still Willy's house, but in the "present." Linda, in Willy's absence, asks Biff why he and Willy hate each other. Biff calls Willy a "fake." (Preparation for the hotel scene.) Linda reveals that Willy has tried to kill himself. (Preparation for Willy's suicide.) Linda declares that Biff is responsible for Willy's life. (This sharpens the conflict between father and son, and shows that there is something vital at stake.) Willy enters. Biff promises again to see Oliver. Linda, however, wonders whether Oliver will recall Biff. (Prep-

aration for the cafe scene.) Upstairs, Willy remembers Biff's
days of glory as a football star. Downstairs, Biff, alone, steps
into the darkened kitchen and lights a cigaret. The tiny spark
of cigaret light is replaced by "a golden pool of light." (This
new light suggests both the moonlight of the "present" and
the sunlight of Ebbets Field in the "past.") Upstairs, Willy
recalls Biff as hero; downstairs, Biff reveals the non-hero. As
Willy declares that such "greatness" as Biff once knew "can
never really fade away," the light on Willy fades—and, in
effect, fades on Willy's "dream." Downstairs, a new light ironically begins to glow—the flame of the gas heater where, according to Linda, Willy had previously attempted suicide. (It is
difficult to place this moment. Although the mood suggests
"simultaneity," it seems, in spite of the lighting and non-
objective glow of the heater "through the kitchen wall," that
the sequence as a whole is closer to the "present.") In the
final thirteen lines of dialogue and stage directions, Miller
foreshadows four events: first, Linda asks Willy what Biff
"has against" him—but she receives no reply (Preparation for
the hotel scene); second, Willy again promises to ask Howard
for a job in New York (Preparation for the scene in Howard's
office); third, Biff is "horrified" by the sight of the rubber
tubing on the heater (Preparation for Willy's suicide and Biff's
reaction); fourth, Willy gazes with wonder at the "moon moving between the buildings." (Preparation for the seemingly
futile "success dream" that finally destroys Willy.) (pp. 160-
172)

ACT TWO

SEVENTH TIME-SEQUENCE. This is the first of six jumps forward in "present" time. It is the following morning in Willy's
house. Willy and Linda are happy. (Preparation by contrast

for the end.) Biff has gone to see Oliver. (Preparation for
the cafe scene.) Willy is going to buy seeds to plant in the
yard. (Preparation for a scene later in the yard.) Willy is
going to ask Howard today for a job in New York. (Preparation.) Linda says that the boys want to treat Willy to a meal
tonight. (Specific preparation for the cafe scene.) One more
payment on the house, says Willy, and the place is ours. (Preparation for Linda's final speech of the play.) Willy observes
Linda mending a silk stocking which makes him "nervous."
(Preparation for the hotel scene where Willy gives the Woman
silk stockings.) Light fades on the house. (pp. 173-176)

EIGHTH TIME-SEQUENCE. This is the second jump forward in
"present" time. Light rises on Howard in his office. Howard
shows more interest in his wire-recording device than in
Willy's plight. Willy reminds Howard of old man Wagner's
"promises," but Howard is ignorant of the past. There is an
argument—and Howard exits. (pp. 177-181)

NINTH TIME-SEQUENCE. Willy, alone in the office, talks to
"Frank Wagner" about his "promises" in the "past." Acci-
dently, Willy trips the machine and the fulfillment of the
"promises" appears in the mechanical, sing-song voice of
Howard's son impersonally reciting the capitals of the forty-
eight states. In terror, Willy screams for Howard to turn off
the machine. (p. 181)

TENTH TIME-SEQUENCE. Howard returns and, in effect, fires
Willy from the firm. Howard exits. (pp. 182-183)

ELEVENTH TIME-SEQUENCE. Willy, alone again in the office,
returns to the "past." Ben enters and advises Willy to quit
selling. Linda, however, appears and encourages Willy. Enter
the boys. Willy argues that he is teaching them how to "succeed." Ben exits, sceptical. Suddenly the Lomans prepare for
Biff's big game in Ebbets Field. Charley and Bernard appear,
and Charley casts doubt on the importance of the game—which
causes Willy to affirm more insistently upon Biff's future

greatness. (This sequence looks back ironically on the preceding sequence, and also points forward toward the following
sequence.) (pp. 183-186)

TWELFTH TIME-SEQUENCE. This is the third jump forward in
"present" time. Light rises on Charley's office. Bernard, a
lawyer now, asks Willy why Biff never succeeded at anything.
When Bernard recalls that summer when Biff returned from
visiting Willy in Boston—claiming that it was then that Biff
had "given up his life"—Willy grows angry and evasive. (Preparation for the hotel scene.) Bernard exits. Willy, borrowing
money from Charley, says: "you end up worth more dead than
alive." (Preparation.) Blackout. (pp. 186-193)

THIRTEENTH TIME-SEQUENCE. Place: the cafe—in the "present." This is the fourth jump forward in time. Biff informs
Happy that Oliver failed to remember him. He then confesses
to having stolen the basketballs years ago, and he also admits
to having stolen Oliver's pen that afternoon. Biff tells Happy
that he no longer feels "spiteful" toward Willy. (Preparation
for the hotel scene.) Happy urges a girl at a nearby table to
call a "friend" for Biff. (Preparation for the sons' abandonment
of Willy in the cafe.) Willy enters. When Biff tries to tell
the "truth," Willy complicates matters by telling the boys that
Howard has fired him. (pp. 193-200)

FOURTEENTH TIME-SEQUENCE. "Simultaneity." While Willy
talks in the "present" with the boys, events of the "past" are
projected across the stage. While Biff struggles to tell the
"truth," Bernard, as a boy, comes to Willy's house and tells
Linda that Biff has failed in math. (Simultaneous juxtaposition of cause and effect.) Bernard informs Linda that Biff
went to see Willy in Boston. (Preparation for the hotel scene,
which will focus the above cause-effect juxtaposition in a new
light.) "Light on house area snaps out." (pp. 200-201)

FIFTEENTH TIME-SEQUENCE. Action resumes wholly in the
"present." Willy is shocked by Biff's confession that he stole
Oliver's pen. (p. 201)

SIXTEENTH TIME-SEQUENCE. "Simultaneity." Over dialogue in the "present," comes the sound of a telephone operator's voice from the "past." (The cafe scene is being played off against the coming scene in the hotel.) While Biff in the "present" says: "Talk to me, Dad," the operator's voice from out of the "past" ironically says: "Mr. Loman does not answer." The laughter of the Woman is also heard. (Preparation for the hotel scene.) Willy strikes Biff. This is the turning point of the play. The girls enter. (Preparation.) Willy exits to the washroom. (pp. 201-204)

SEVENTEENTH TIME-SEQUENCE. Action resumes in the "present." Biff accuses Happy of not being concerned about Willy: "He's going to kill himself, don't you know that?" (Preparation.) Biff exits; and Happy follows with the girls. (pp. 204-205)

EIGHTEENTH TIME-SEQUENCE. Place: the washroom in the cafe. Time: the "past." Willy reconstructs the scene in the Boston hotel. Biff, eighteen, appears in Willy's room and informs his father that he has failed math. Suddenly the Woman enters from Willy's bedroom, looking for her silk stockings. Biff's idealized image of his father is suddenly destroyed. Calling Willy a "fake," Biff vows never to go to college—which, in effect, is a vow never to succeed in life. (pp. 205-208)

NINETEENTH TIME-SEQUENCE. In the "present," Willy is helped from the cafe by a waiter. Willy exits, looking for a hardware store where he can purchase seeds. (Preparation.) (p. 209)

TWENTIETH TIME-SEQUENCE. This is the fifth jump forward in the "present." Time: later the same evening. Place: Willy's house. Linda attacks Biff and Happy for having abandoned Willy in the cafe. "Hammering is heard from outside the house. . . ." Linda and Biff move toward Willy, who is in the yard. (Preparation for the final encounter between Willy and Biff.) (pp. 210-212)

TWENTY-FIRST TIME-SEQUENCE: Place: the yard. Time: the

"past." While Willy is planting seeds, Ben appears, and Willy reveals his suicide plans. (Preparation.) With the insurance money in his hands, Willy argues, Biff will see again that his father was really "number one." Ben warns Willy, however, that Biff will call him a "fool" and a "coward." (Preparation for the Requiem.) (pp. 212-213)

TWENTY-SECOND TIME-SEQUENCE. In the "present," Willy and Biff argue—the action moving from the yard to the house. Biff says that he is leaving forever. Willy calls it "spite." Biff shows Willy the rubber tubing, and declares that if Willy destroys himself there will be no pity forthcoming from his beloved son. (Preparation.) Biff claims that the Lomans have been self-deceived for years—Willy pretending to be a great salesman when he was nothing but a "hard-working drummer who landed in the ash can," while Biff himself was strictly "one dollar an hour." But Willy insists on the greatness of the Lomans. Enraged, Biff attacks his father, but is suddenly overcome with tenderness and, sobbing, says: "Will you take that phony dream and burn it before something happens?" To Willy, this is proof of Biff's love. (The Crisis of the play.) (pp. 213-218)

TWENTY-THIRD TIME-SEQUENCE: "Simultaneity." While Willy talks in the "present" to Linda and Happy, Ben appears "just outside the kitchen." Says Willy: "I always knew . . . we were gonna make it, Biff and I." (Preparation.) Willy recalls Biff's days of glory as a football star. (Points back toward the curtain of Act One.) It is clear now that Willy will kill himself. (Points back to the beginning of the play.) Over Linda's frantic appeals, Willy exits. The roar of Willy's car is heard, carrying the salesman to his death. (The Climax of the play.) (pp. 218-220)

TWENTY-FOURTH TIME-SEQUENCE. This is the sixth and last jump forward in the "present." It is the following day, or perhaps several days later. Linda, Biff, Happy, Charley, and Bernard move slowly "through the wall-line of the kitchen" to the apron of the stage, gazing down at Willy's "grave." (Preparation for the Requiem.) (p. 220)

REQUIEM *its musical setting*

Biff says that Willy "had the wrong dreams." (Points back.) Happy argues that Willy's "dream" was right. (Points back.) Linda says: "I made the last payment on the house today . . . and there'll be nobody home." (Points back.) (The Conclusion of the play.) (pp. 221-222)

Before further discussion of the time-sequences, a brief look at certain technical devices—namely, Miller's use of lights and sound in the play—is in order, in an effort to determine whether the "internal" has been satisfactorily integrated with the "external."

Lighting performs three major functions in the play. First, light serves as a transitional device; it moves the action from place to place in the "present," but it also signals shifts in point of view—quite often, for example, the movement from objective to subjective is effected by the "green light of leaves" falling (pp. 142, 200, 220). The reverse movement is accomplished by either dimming the lights (p. 151) or by abrupt blackout (p. 201). The method is not arbitrary, for the mood of a specific scene determines the technique employed. Secondly, light functions as ironic comment on the action. (The ending of Act One is an example.) Finally, light functions, as has already been suggested, as mood-inspiring. (These categories overlap, of course.) The hostile city, for instance, appears as "an angry glow of orange" (p. 130); the cafe appears in a "red glow" (p. 193); and Willy's attempt to plant seeds in his yard is covered by the tender "blue of night" (p. 212).

Similarly, sound has three chief functions. First, sound is used to characterize. The best illustration here is Willy's theme —the sound of the flute. The play opens and closes with Willy's theme, hence the flute acts as a kind of auditory binder. The flute tells of "grass and trees and the horizon" (p. 130), ironically juxtaposing in Willy's mind the promise of the past with the actuality of the present. Since Willy's father made flutes, the sound points back toward Willy's childhood—thus the music helps to give Willy an added dimension. The flute also characterizes Willy in another way, for it comes to suggest his suicidal impulses. Early in the play, Willy discovers his mistake in thinking he had opened the windshield on his new car: "He breaks off in amazement and fright as the flute is heard distinctly" (p. 136). When the action moves from the cafe to the house for the final scene "the sound of the flute" comes up over the darkened stage (p. 209). And, lastly, when, in the Requiem, Linda "searches" for an answer to Willy's death, once again the sound of the flute is heard (p. 222). The other characters have their music, too: the music of the boys is "gay" (p. 184); Ben's theme is "idyllic" (p. 218); and Willy's father's theme is "a high, rollicking tune" (p. 157). The second chief function of sound is as ironic comment on the action. The "gay and bright" music of the boys, which opens Act Two, contrasts with the monotonous drone of Howard's machine in the following scene. Ben's music, which opens the scene after the one in Howard's office, contrasts with the traffic sounds that rise up from the street into Charley's office in the following scene. This alternation and juxtaposition of sound has obvious thematic relevance. The third function of sound is to establish mood: the "mocking frenzy" that closes the subjective sequence in Howard's office, for example (p. 186); the "raucous music" that opens the cafe scene (p. 193); the "raw, sensuous music" that underscores the scene in the hotel (p. 205)—the last two examples reveal how Miller has ironically linked the promiscuity of the boys to Willy's failure as a husband and father.

The foregoing discussion of *Death of a Salesman* shows clearly that its structure is highly integrated. Exposition is continual and always relevant to action and theme; the time-sequences reveal the amazing number of preparations for coming events. The final scene of Act One is a masterpiece of constructive art. There is no inconsequential byplay in *Salesman*; no loss of focus on the protagonist; no hidden letter tricks; and no "jumps." Action rises smoothly, steadily, and convincingly. If space permitted, a good deal might be added to what has already been suggested about the uses of irony in the play—a sure sign of Miller's increasing sophistication and restraint.

In general, point of view alternates consistently between the objective and the subjective. A few inconsistencies, however, are evident. The Requiem seems to be the one serious violation of the conventions previously esablished in the play. Once Willy is dead there would appear to be no authority for the alternation of sequences, for Willy, as the Jamesian "commanding center," is the sole warrant for, and subject of, the transitions from objective to subjective point of view. Yet at the end of Act Two after Willy's death, the "leaves of day" appear and the characters "move . . . through the wall-line of the kitchen" (p. 220). As Miller himself says, however, this device is reserved for the "past" (p. 131). The dream-like air that surrounds the opening scene before Willy appears is, on the other hand, perhaps defensible. Willy is alive and the reader can presume (but only reflexively) that this is Willy's view of the house as he enters the opening scene (much like the subjective camera technique in cinema). Lack of fixtures does not clearly signal anything, since selective realism and expressionism may touch here. It is doubtful whether anything could be devised that would render perfectly clear, at the outset, the mode of imitation in *Salesman*, simply because the mode alternates. This is a minor problem. There is no reason to confuse Miller's method, as critics have done, with the flashback technique; it is difficult to see how the card-playing scene in Act One, for example, could be confused with a flashback when "present" and "past" are obviously being projected simultaneously. Ben,

Ben

however, presents a different problem. He is the one character in the play who is never revealed in an objective manner; that is, Ben is never viewed by the audience apart from Willy's imaginative reconstruction of him. This fact, however, does not acquit Miller of a certain lack of consistency in imitation. Intrinsically, Ben's appearance in the "subjective" and "subjective-objective" sequences are no different in kind from the appearances of the other characters. All of the characters in these sequences, as I have insisted, are imaginative reconstructions by Willy, and as such should be formalized in *some way or other*, as Ben is formalized when re-created by Willy. In the "subjective" portions of the play, however, there is little or no increase in formalization of either character or language.

It seems inconsistent to applaud the logic of the structure and at the same time minimize the devices that permit the concrete enactment of the logic. *Death of a Salesman* is, as my analysis has shown, highly unified. Light and sound are major contributions to the "sensuous" quality missing from Miller's earlier works but manifest in *Salesman*. Only one or two criticisms are in order. Since the flute sound has its origin inside Willy's head, the sound falls under the same censure as point of view in the Requiem. Should Miller have sacrificed dramatic effect for consistency? The play might very well be stronger (and a discussion of theme will underline this observation) had Miller eliminated the Requiem entirely. One might also quibble over the music that introduces the cafe scene, since (once more) Willy is not present to give authority to the sound. There is, however, one possible exception. The fade-in, fade-out technique seems to be on a different level from, say, the "green leaves" of Willy's past. One might argue that in the age of film, audiences have come to accept cinematic dissolves with accompanying music. Music in *Salesman*, however, is highly individualized, extremely selective, and well-integrated with action and theme, and, hence, there would seem to be some doubt whether the argument from film is valid. One cannot be too dogmatic on these matters—otherwise one might also object to the skeleton set itself, which in the objective scenes is taken to be perfectly "natural" by one and all in the play. Taken as a whole—and considering the extreme difficulty of the enterprise—structure in *Death of a Salesman* is remarkably consistent and unified.

But are the characters of the play complex and consistent in a way that parallels the structure?

Physically, Willy Loman is not described in detail: "He is past sixty years of age, dressed quietly . . . [and] his exhaustion is apparent" (p. 131); but there is contrast here, for Willy—who stresses "appearances"—is simply not physically "impressive." Sociologically, Willy belongs to the lower-middle class. Dialogue reveals that he is a traveling salesman from Brooklyn, who has averaged seventy to one hundred dollars a week for a period of over thirty years, but to earn such money, Willy must "be at it ten, twelve hours a day" (p. 149). Willy's job has no built-in security against old age. Through dialogue, Miller creates a sense of the past. Willy became a salesman because in the early days selling seemed to possess "comradeship" and real "personality" (pp. 180-181), but selling has changed in thirty years, and Willy cannot adjust to the changes. Not that Willy was ever a great salesman, even in the early days (p. 181). Actually, Willy would probably have been happier as a carpenter, although in the play he takes a superior stance toward "mere" carpentering (p. 166). Willy seems to have had little education; his father was always on the move, "he'd toss the whole family into the wagon, and then he'd drive the team right across the country" (p. 157). There is no religion in Willy's life, no philosophical system to sustain him, and no political convictions to absorb or direct his energy. Willy believes everything he reads in the newspaper—even the advertisements (p. 148). Willy Loman is "low-man": the alienated, hypersensitive, urbanized cipher of modern society. Psychologically, Willy has many traits. He appreciates nature (p. 132),

and he is often nostalgic (p. 135). He is both dependent on
Linda and domineering toward her (pp. 134-135). (He reveals
the same pattern with Charley.) Willy is persistent—he "can't
walk away" (p. 190). He is clearly gullible. His father, who is
held up as a "real man," actually abandoned his family to
search for gold in Alaska and this abandonment has left Willy
with deep feelings of insecurity (p. 159). Consequently, Willy
feels the need to overcompensate by being "number-one." His
dominant trait, then, is a restless ambition for "success." Willy
tends to exaggerate; his moods swing abruptly (pp. 147-148).
Although Willy has been sexually unfaithful to Linda, he is no
callous profligate. He feels deep remorse. Clearly, then, Willy
has a tender conscience. This sensitivity is also manifest in
Willy's frustration over not having attained his idealized image
of himself—and over Biff's not having attained Willy's idealized
image of Biff. The inner contradiction that drives Willy to self-
destruction is the need to prove his worth against the fear
that he has failed as both a father and a salesman: "I am not a
dime a dozen! I am Willy Loman, and you are Biff Loman!"
(p. 217)

Biff is described in this manner:

> Biff is two years older than his brother Happy [that is,
> thirty-four], well built, but in these days bears a worn
> air and seems less self-assured. He has succeeded less,
> and his dreams are stronger and less acceptable than
> Happy's. (p. 136)

After his days of high school football glory, things changed
for Biff:

> I spent six or seven years after high school trying to
> work myself up. Shipping clerk, salesman, business of
> one kind or another. And it's a measly manner of ex-
> istence . . . when all you really desire is to be out-

doors. . . . And still—that's how you build a future.
(p. 138)

Dialogue also illuminates Biff's hopes for the future: "with a
ranch I could do the work I like and still be something" (p.
141); it also reveals how Biff comes to reject that "something":

What am I doing in [Oliver's] office, making a con-
temptuous, begging fool of myself, when all I want is out
[West], waiting for me the minute I say I know who I
am! (p. 217)

Biff is rich in traits: he is moody (p. 133); he is a petty, com-
pulsive thief (p. 141)—which suggests that Biff feels unloved
for what he is in himself; he is spiteful (p. 215); he is proud
(p. 216); he is self-deceived (p. 197); he suffers from self-
contempt (p. 211). Unlike Willy, however, Biff has the
capacity to face the truth about himself (p. 216). Biff's
dominant trait, in fact, is his restless search for self-identity.
His inner contradiction is precisely his ambivalent attitude
toward his father. Thus, he tells the girl in the cafe that Willy
is:

A fine, troubled prince. A hardworking unappreciated
prince. A pal . . . a good companion. Always for his
boys. (p. 204)

But he tells Willy:

I never got anywhere because you blew me so full of hot
air I could never stand taking orders from anybody!
That's whose fault it is! (p. 216)

The contradiction results in Biff's paralyzing confusion: "I
don't know—what I'm supposed to want" (p. 138).

None of the other characters in *Salesman* has the complexity of Willy and Biff. All of them are very nearly dominated by a single trait: Happy is selfish, Linda is unselfish, Ben is confident, Howard is callous, Bernard is steady, and Charley is "mature." Similarly, the minor characters are static. Are Willy and Biff static? Willy certainly arrives at a mild condemnation of selling when, in regard to his suicide plan and the resultant insurance money, he tells Ben: "This would not be another damned-fool appointment. . . ." (p. 213). He also comes to see that Biff truly loves him (p. 218). Basically, however, Willy remains the same throughout the play—and this, of course, would seem to be Miller's point. Character growth— William Archer preferred "disclosure"—is only a means to an end. We can believe in static Willy in a way we cannot believe in "jumping" Joe Keller. Biff, on the other hand, definitely grows, for he achieves a number of insights that culminate in a major development in self-awareness. Biff sees, for example, that he was self-deceived about Oliver (p. 197); he sees how all the Lomans have been self-deceived (p. 216); and he stops his "spiteful" behavior toward Willy and relinquishes the "phony dream" (p. 217), thus accepting the "reality" of himself (p. 222).

It has been said that Biff, not Willy, is the protagonist in *Salesman*. If we consider the action of the play, however, and not preconceived and arbitrary criteria, it is easy to see why Willy, not Biff, is the protagonist. It is Willy who forces the conflict; Willy who cannot surrender his "dream"; Willy who will not allow Biff to rest in his "failure"; Willy who asks Howard for a job in New York; Willy who is unfaithful to Linda; Willy who borrows money from Charley; Willy who pursues Ben for the "answer"; and Willy who destroys himself in order to be "number-one."

Finally, the unity of opposites in the play is binding. Compromise is impossible between Willy and Biff, both men being what they are and desiring different things. (Compromise is also impossible between Willy and the "system"—what Willy wants, even only a "little salary," and what Howard will give him—"I can't take blood from a stone"—are opposed.) What makes the unity binding is the simple fact that Willy "can't walk away" from Biff. (Willy, it is true, could take a job from Charley, but he is too proud to admit defeat—and it is his pride that drives him to suicide.)

The above discussion should make plain that Willy and Biff are three-dimensional characters. Structurally, as we have seen, dialogue performs its office through expert exposition and foreshadowing. Here, in terms of character, dialogue is made to reveal as much of the past, present, and future of Willy and Biff as is necessary for a proper understanding of the action. In short, dialogue in *Salesman* is extremely functional. One reason why Willy is more alive than Joe Keller is the fact that dialogue is more specific about Willy—we learn more about the salesman, such as, his important childhood environment (which helps us to understand his adult behavior) or that he lives in Brooklyn, New York (which helps us to place him within a concrete context and also to make allowances for his speech patterns). The more we know about Willy, the more interest we have in his fate. The fact that Miller starts the point of attack with Willy already an attempted suicide, with the focus steadily on Willy as the protagonist, and with Willy's inner contradictions continually on view, permits us to believe in Willy and his death in a way that was impossible in the case of Joe Keller.

There is no denying, however, that something is lacking in the minor characters. One might argue that Willy and Biff are at the center of things, that they are sufficiently delineated, and that there is no necessity for the other characters to be fully drawn. There is some truth in such an argument, for every play requires flat characters. Charley, Bernard, Howard, and Ben are perhaps "there" enough for the parts they are to enact. Eric Bentley has asked whether Ben is "more than a

sentimental motif?" Since Ben is seen in the play by Willy
alone, and since Willy is sentimental about Ben, the answer
to Bentley seems obvious. But Bentley's charge that Willy's
marriage is not "*there* for us to inspect and understand down
to its depths" is less easy to counter. Although Miller's concern
is with Willy and Biff, not Willy and Linda, the fact remains
that Linda is more flat than would seem either desirable or
necessary. To a lesser extent, the same criticism might be scored
against Happy. A play, however, is not judged by its characters
alone, for every element in a play is part of a total design, and
characters are evaluated in respect to how well they contribute
to that design. Characterization—including the controversial
question of Willy's qualifications for a tragic role—can be
viewed in more depth, then, against a background of theme
in Miller's play.

Critics of *Death of a Salesman,* when they have not been
vexed by the problem of genre—a problem that will be taken
up at the end of this chapter—have most often been concerned
with two aspects of the theme: 1) unity of conception; and
2) the values inherent in Miller's "counterweight" to Willy
Loman's "wrong dreams."

Is the "system" to blame for Willy's fate, ask some critics,
or is the fault within Willy's character? Is there a "split" here
between "personal" (or "Freudian") and "social" (or "Marx-
ian") motivation? Moreover, Miller's "positive" values, some
critics urge, reveal a "romantic" and "sentimental" view of
man—that is, Biff's emphasis on "freedom and the body,"
"self-realization," and "the simple life" are "romantic" and
"sentimental"—while the references to Willy's working with
his hands is an inadequate solution to the problems posed by
the play. Few Americans, it has also been alleged, believe with
Willy Loman that success depends on being "well liked."

Criticism of thematic unity in *Salesman,* it is obvious,
betrays a curious "either-or" kind of thinking. Usually Miller is
pummelled for too overtly trying to "prove the theme," but

with *Salesman* the strategy has been to attack him for being too "realistic." Actually Miller should be praised for having succeeded in the difficult task of integrating the "personal" and the "social" in his play. Notice, for example, that Biff more than once calls Willy a "fake." Although this word has a double reference in the play, thematically it is all of a piece. Willy is a "fake" for being unfaithful to Linda; he is also a "fake" as a salesman, for he is nothing but an unsuccessful "drummer." Moreover, Willy's values are "fake," since they stem from his "phony dream." Nor is Willy's infidelity merely "personal"—it results from his loneliness (loneliness which has a "social" dimension, since it is a necessary concomitant of his work role) and his anxiety to keep ahead of other salesmen in a competitive society. The hotel scene is central because it crystallizes for Biff, Willy's essential falseness; that is, it leads to Biff's questioning of *all* Willy's values, and his eventual rejection of them. True, Biff would probably have "failed" (however defined) in business anyway; but the hotel scene is also linked to the play's climax, for Biff's insight into Willy and his "spiteful" attitude toward him is a preparation for his insight into himself and his subsequent acceptance of himself. To ask a modern dramatist to write a play that emphasizes *either* social necessity *or* individual responsibility would seem to involve an oversimplified approach to experience. The abstract discussion of freedom versus determinism, usually conducted in a philosophical vacuum, seems ultimately a deadend; in actuality, we recognize the rival claims of both factors, and we manage to live with both. As in *All My Sons*, Miller appears to affirm freedom at the same time that he underlines the influence of social forces. A Charley can remain fundamentally decent in spite of the negative elements in society. A Ben (at least Willy's version of Ben) can succeed ruthlessly, but remain self-assured and apparently free from guilt. The same might be said of Howard. Willy, on the other hand, loses his way in such a world—and who can determine the exact degree of his culpability? (In Nazi Germany, although some men lost their integrity, some men did not; but it does not follow that there were no evil forces in German society.) How separate the "social" from the "personal" in *Salesman?* Willy, for example, has deep-rooted feelings of insecurity: "Dad left when I was such a baby and . . . I still feel—kind of temporary about myself" (p. 159). This sounds "personal." But would Willy have felt so "temporary" in a society that offered more community, more "comradeship"? Surely it is trite to observe that a society such as ours, with shifting social values, hardly furnishes an ideal structure for self-discovery. *Death of a Salesman* reflects the density and complexity of life itself. Why then must we choose either "personal" or "social," either "political" or "sexual" explanations? Why "Freudianism" or "Marxism"? "Freudianism" and "Marxism" are, like *Salesman,* abstractions from life; but if "Freudianism" and "Marxism" are "total ideologies" and "mutually exclusive," that does not mean that *Salesman* cannot use both "ideologies," for a play does not project "total ideologies" (except thesis plays), but assimilates "totalities" to its own unique pattern and design.

In the Requiem, Miller seems quite explicit about what "wrong dreams" possessed Willy; Happy says: "[Willy] had a good dream. It's the only dream you can have—to come out number-one man" (p. 222). Why must Charley necessarily speak for Miller? (Are we always sure who speaks for Shakespeare?) It is not true that the scene as a whole speaks of *the* salesman; only Charley speaks of *the* salesman—the other characters speak of Willy. And the answer to, Who was Willy? is suggested in Biff's remark that "There's more of [Willy] in that front stoop than in all the sales he ever made" (p. 221); it is implied in Happy's statement (above), for Willy was less than the "number-one man"; and Willy, like Biff (Miller seems to imply), should have accepted his limitations. Biff's objection to Willy appears to be that Willy defines himself too narrowly in terms of his social role. Is Charley's definition of Willy in respect to *the* salesman confusing? Is Charley out of character here? Miller says: "In all [Charley] says, despite what he says, there is pity. . . ." (p. 152). In the action of the play, Charley speaks hard: "When a deposit bottle is broken you don't get your nickle back" (p. 154); "My salvation is that I never took any interest in anything" (p. 191); "The only thing you got in this world is what you can sell" (p. 192). Yet Charley comes in the middle of the night to cheer Willy; he "lends" Willy fifty dollars a week; and he endures Willy's insults for years. This shows that Charley is not so hard as he pretends, that we need not take at face value all that he says. Aside from this, there seems to be no necessary inconsistency in Charley's Requiem speech. Previously, Charley has said that—in the broad sense—we are all salesmen; what he has debunked throughout the play is Willy's belief in "personality" ("Who liked J. P. Morgan?" asks Charley [p. 192]). In his farewell to Willy, however, perhaps out of his characteristic pity, he seems to be softening his previous debunking, he seems to be saying that so long as there *are* salesmen—in the narrow sense now—then *that* kind of "salesman is got to dream. . . . It comes with the territory" (p. 222). Charley would seem, then, to be merely "realistic." Moreover, perhaps a part of Charley's function in the Requiem is to speak only good of the dead, in an effort to hearten Willy's widow. If this reading is valid, Charley remains in character.

It is difficult, however, to justify Linda's final speech: "Why did you do it? I search and search and I search, and I can't understand it, Willy" (p. 222). True, even an expected event might cause surprise—rational understanding cannot prevent emotional shock, especially in the case of a loved one's suicide. Linda, moreover, being sympathetic but not very perceptive, could never enter wholly into Willy's dreams—she was different in that she could "walk away" ("life is a casting off," she says, p. 133). Nevertheless, one feels that there is a spurious element here—an abandonment of logic for the sake of a "curtain." Linda knew of Willy's previous suicide attempts; she knew of his depression over Biff and the job; and she knew a great deal about Willy's dreams. There would seem to be very little, really, to search for on Linda's part. The one thing that Linda knew nothing about was Willy's infidelity; but Willy's infidelity was not causally related to his suicide. In spite of the fact that much of the specific content of the Requiem is defensible, however, it still seems unsatisfactory. Technically, as has been said, it violates the convention of point of view, and, although it helps to focus the theme, it says nothing really new, nothing that has not been better expressed in the previous action. Moreover, in its final utterance, it is even somewhat specious and confusing.

With such terms in mind as "freedom and the body," "self-realization," and "the simple life," a reading of Plato's *Republic* might suggest that the Greeks, far from being "classical," were in reality extremely "romantic." The "classical-romantic" dichotomy thus becomes semantically meaningless. Equally unsatisfactory are vague terms like "nature" and "individualism." The critical question is whether Miller has rendered a complex vision of experience, not whether the critic necessarily agrees with the alleged interpretation of the vision. The play implies that Willy might have been happier in a pre-"capitalistic" (or perhaps pre-industrial) society; it more plainly suggests that Willy would have been happier working with his "hands"; and it makes manifest that Biff feels that—*for him*—the West is the answer. Psychologically, it is a truism to say that a man will be happy doing what he can do best. What appears to disturb some critics is that this "answer" is not "profound" enough. Would Oedipus have brought on his fate if he had not been rash? Would Lear have ended badly had he not been short-tempered? How "profound" are the specific "counter-weights" here? Moreover, is Miller offering a "universal" solution to a modern problem? Obviously not; not all men are good with their "hands" (Charley, for example [p. 154]); and it is

precisely the point that Biff's "solution" is unique—doesn't
he say: "I know who I am"? (p. 222). Biff speaks for Biff.
Furthermore, *Salesman* raises questions that can never be
answered in a scientific way. Was it really "better" in pre-
"capitalistic" America? Historically, of course, the economic
and social transformation of American society had already
begun when, in terms of the play, Willy's father sold flutes
across the country. *In terms of the play*, however, there is no
"proof" that Miller is "saying" that pre-"capitalistic" society
was "better"—for the contrast between "past" and "present"
is limited by point of view, and the "past" is wholly Willy's
projection. As for the positive values that seem to emerge from
the play—"romantic" and "sentimental" values—one might
fairly ask whether they are quite so shoddy as some critics
would have us believe. These same critics would have to hold
(and perhaps some do) that the democratic experiment is
shoddy, that it is "romantic" and "sentimental," since these
same values are part of the democratic rhetoric. Not all of us,
however, have lost faith in that rhetoric. *Salesman* also poses
questions which, it is hoped, are answerable, but which as yet
have not been answered—such as, how are we to reconcile
human values with an expanding economy of abundance which
puts a premium on mechanization and impersonality? Critics
who assault *Salesman* rarely reveal where *they* stand; they
seem to suggest that the answer has been found—perhaps
they themselves have the answer—but that Miller, through
sheer stupidity or perversity, has not provided the answer.
Some critics miss the theological and metaphysical dimension
in *Salesman*; but in a pluralistic society such as ours it is surely
arrogant to demand a single standard.

Death of a Salesman possesses both "particular" and "universal" features. How many Americans believe in being "well
liked"? (It should be pointed out here that Willy Loman
works hard, too—ten to twelve hours a day, in fact.) According to C. Wright Mills, our society places an increasing

importance on "personality." A survey taken by one American
university discovered that college graduates with "personality"
would be more readily hired than other graduates, even if
those others had higher grades, the only exceptions being in
the scientific and technical fields; but in all other areas such
qualities as skill, aptitude, creativeness, are merely subordinate
to "appearance" and "personality." As Mills sees it the troubles
of white-collar people are universal ones in our time. One might
add, however, that Willy's troubles are not limited to the
twentieth century. To take but one approach, the use of the
flute in *Salesman* suggests a passage in Thoreau's *Walden*
which I do not believe any critic has noticed. Discussing
"John Farmer," who "heard some one playing on a flute and
that sound harmonized with his mood," Thoreau says:

> But the notes of the flute came home to his ears out of a
> different sphere from that he worked in, and suggested
> work for certain faculties which slumbered in him. They
> gently did away with the street, and the village, and
> the state in which he lived. A voice said to him,—Why
> do you stay here and live this mean moiling life, when a
> glorious existence is possible for you? Those same stars
> twinkle over other fields than these.—But how to come
> out of this condition and actually migrate thither?
> All that he could think of was to practice some new
> austerity, to let his mind descend into his body and
> redeem it, and treat himself with ever increasing respect.

Whether Miller had this passage in mind is irrelevant; the
similar use of the flute in both works suggests a "universal"
situation—since Thoreau was writing about "John Farmer" and
not, like Miller, about a modern huckster, "Willy Loman."
This problem of universality raises a question about Miller's
play that has usurped all other problems in the minds of some
critics.

I refer, of course, to the question about whether or not *Death of a Salesman* is a "true" tragedy. Is Willy Loman a "true" tragic hero? Does Willy have stature? Does he achieve "insight"? How representative is he? These, for some minds, have been the burning critical questions.

Nor has Miller himself been unconcerned with the dispute. In "Tragedy and the Common Man" (*Theatre Arts, XXXV* [March 1951], 48-50), Miller expounds *his* theory of tragedy. "In the tragic view," says Miller, "the need of man to wholly realize himself is the only fixed star. . . ." The tragic hero, for Miller, "is intent on claiming his whole due as a personality." Says Miller:

> the fateful wound from which the inevitable events spiral is the wound of indignity, and its dominant force is indignation. Tragedy, then, is the consequence of a man's total compulsion to evaluate himself justly.

The tragic flaw is the hero's "inherent unwillingness to remain passive in the face of what he conceives to be a challenge to his dignity," and "his destruction in the attempt posits a wrong or an evil in his environment." But the "possibility of victory must be there," or, according to Miller, there is pathos and not tragedy. Miller argues that his view of tragedy is ample enough to embrace the common man. In the "Introduction" to the *Collected Plays* Miller, as Emile McAnany has shown, develops his conception of tragedy further. A new emphasis is placed on the tragic hero's commitment to a set of values which he cannot relinquish. This new emphasis, moreover, is at the expense of Miller's previous insistence on the evil in the hero's environment.

Critics, at least those bound by "traditional" standards of tragedy, have not accepted either Miller's theory or his play as "true." Miller himself, it should be noted, has expressed dissatisfaction with Willy's lack of insight (*Theatre Arts,*

XXXVII [October 1953], 34). After reading through all that
has been written on this subject, however, one is tempted to
dismiss the tedious discussion by roundly declaring that *Death
of a Salesman* is a moving and powerful play, and thus it is
irrelevant whether or not Miller has written a "true" tragedy.
If the "traditionalist" standard is the only acceptable one for
tragedy, then it is plain that *Salesman* is no tragedy. For no
one would claim for Willy a profound intelligence, and if
stature is dependent on intelligence, Willy falls short of tragic
grandeur. Miller's admission that Willy lacks sufficient insight
plays into the hands of hostile critics. It is true that Willy
does lack the degree of insight achieved by, say, King Lear.
Nevertheless, it seems to me that Miller is correct when, in
his "Introduction," he argues:

> Had Willy been unaware of his separation from values
> that endure he would have died contentedly while polish-
> ing his car. . . . But he was agonized by his awareness
> of being in a false position. . . . That he had not the
> intellectual fluency to verbalize his situation is not the
> same thing as saying that he lacked awareness, even an
> overly intensified consciousness that the life he had
> made was without form and inner meaning. (pp. 34-35)

At the end of the play, as I pointed out in my discussion
of character, Willy finds that Biff loves him, though he cannot,
of course, relinquish his dream of making Biff "number-one."
This can be seen as another important, though not ultimately
transforming, insight in *Salesman*. Willy is not given "intellectual fluency" but perhaps Miller has achieved something better,
or at least something just as good—namely, he has shown how
"insight" is warded off, how it is suppressed or repressed, but
how it will not disappear, how it continues to torment the
conscious mind and will, marking its victim as a neurotic and
possibly even a psychotic. Freud has taught our century to re-

think its definitions of "consciousness" (for the "unconscious mind" seems like a contradiction in terms); perhaps it behooves drama critics to redefine their conception of "insight."

It is, I think, sheer obscurantism to dismiss *Salesman*, as some critics from the upper stratosphere have done, because it deals with a "superficial" American environment. Miller treats one phase of our modern world, and he treats it in a powerful and memorable manner. To demand that a playwright project some meaningful order that would satisfy *all* readers is to ask for an intellectual feat that other artists, not to say philosophers, have failed to achieve. If it is true, as C. Wright Mills predicts, that before long all societies will be organized as ours is presently fashioned, then the "universality" of *Salesman* is guaranteed. True, *Salesman* may be "low" tragedy; but it may also be more moving *as a play* than most "high" tragedies. The appreciation of *Salesman*, then, would not seem to depend on whether or not it is a "true" tragedy. This much should be obvious, yet certain critics have seemingly set themselves resolutely against the obvious. Actually, the quarrel over genre may not be an aesthetic one at all; perhaps it really reflects a deep reluctance on the part of "traditional" critics to come to grips with the dark and difficult nature of contemporary experience.

CHAPTER THREE

The Crucible

In *The Crucible* (1953), a four-act play, Miller's scene is Salem, Massachusetts in the year 1692 and the action is based on the witchcraft trials of that time. In "A Note on the Historical Accuracy of This Play," Miller says: "This play is not history in the sense . . . used by the academic historian," for "dramatic purposes" prompted certain changes in the record. Nevertheless, Miller believes the "reader will discover here the essential nature" of the Salem trials (p. 224).

In his "Introduction," Miller recalls his mood at the time of writing the play:

> If the reception of *All My Sons* and *Death of a Salesman* had made the world a friendly place for me, events of the early fifties quickly turned that warmth into an illusion. It was not only the rise of "McCarthyism" that moved me, but something which seemed much more weird and mysterious. It was the fact that a political, objective, knowledgeable campaign from the far Right was capable of creating not only a terror, but a new subjective reality, a veritable mystique which was gradually assuming even a holy resonance. . . . That so interior and subjective an emotion could have been so manifestly created from without was a marvel to me. It underlies every word in *The Crucible*. (pp. 39-40)

Yet, says Miller, he would not have written the play had he "not come upon a single fact," namely, that a young girl, Abigail Williams, "the prime mover of the Salem hysteria, so far as the hysterical children were concerned," who had worked for John and Elizabeth Proctor, had accused Elizabeth of witchcraft but refused "to include John . . . in her accusations despite the urgings of the prosecutors" (p. 41). In short, Miller thought he detected a sexual motive in Abigail's "fastidiousness" toward John which "made the play conceivable for" him. (p. 42)

In another passage, Miller relates how his interpretation of the trials affected the structure of *The Crucible*:

> As in any such mass phenomenon, the number of characters of vital, if not decisive, importance is so great as to make the dramatic problem excessively difficult. For a time it seemed best to approach the town impressionistically; and, by a mosaic of seemingly disconnected scenes, gradually to form a context of cause and effect. This I believe I might well have done had it not been that the central impulse for writing at all was not the social but the interior psychological question . . . of that guilt residing in Salem which the hysteria merely unleashed, but did not create. Consequently, the structure reflects that understanding, and it centers in John, Elizabeth, and Abigail. ("Introduction," p. 42)

Enough has been said about Miller's "intentions"; it is time, now, to discuss "achievement" in *The Crucible*. I wish to devote a detailed paragraph to each of Miller's four acts in an effort to trace the line of development, giving particular attention to the point of attack, complication, the turning point, and crisis, climax, and conclusion.

Act One, which Miller calls an "Overture," occurs in the spring of 1692. The scene is the "small upper bedroom" of the

Reverend Samuel Parris. When the curtain rises, Parris is discovered kneeling beside the bed of his daughter, Betty, aged ten, who is suffering from a strange illness. Tituba, Parris's Negro slave is introduced, and her abrupt dismissal by Parris suggests that there is a tension in the household, perhaps even a suspicion that Tituba is related in some way to Betty's illness. On what is actually the first page of dialogue, Abigail enters and relates that, according to the doctor, Betty might be suffering from something "unnatural." Parris, realizing that an "unnatural" influence would reflect on his household, had anticipated the doctor's opinion and sent for an "expert" in demonology—the Reverend Hale—in order to prove that Betty is not possessed. Parris then confronts Abigail, who is his niece, with a serious charge: he claims to have seen Betty, Abigail, Tituba, and other girls dancing in the woods—and, worst of all, one of the girls was naked. Abigail insists that it was a joke, and not a devilish conjuring. Parris reminds his niece that he has enemies, people who wish to drive him from his pulpit. At stake, then, is Parris's job, and perhaps Betty's life. A crucial element in the plot structure is introduced in the following exchange between Parris and Abigail:

> Parris . . . : Abigail, is there any other cause than you have told me, for your being discharged from Goody Proctor's service? I have heard it said . . . that she comes so rarely to the church this year for she will not sit so close to something soiled. . . .
>
> Abigail: She hates me, uncle . . . for I would not be her slave. It's a bitter woman, a lying, cold, sniveling woman, and I will not work for such a woman!
>
> Parris: She may be. And yet it has troubled me that you are now seven months out of their house, and in all this time no other family has ever called for your service.
>
> Abigail, *in a temper*: My name is good in the village! I will not have it said my name is soiled! . . . (p. 232)

The exchange is interrupted by the appearance of Mr. and Mrs. Putnam, both of whom are convinced that witchcraft is operating in Salem. Under repeated questioning, Abigail finally weakens and admits that Tituba was conjuring in the woods. After the adults exit, Mary Warren, the Proctors' eighteen-year-old servant, joins the other girls and accuses Abigail of drinking chicken blood in the woods as a charm to kill Elizabeth Proctor. Abigail threatens to kill the girls if they expose her. (This is the eighth page of dialogue.) John Proctor enters and, after having angrily driven Mary back to work, is alone with Abigail (save for the unconscious Betty) in an expository scene which reveals the couple's past sexual relations. It is clear that Abigail still desires John, and, in spite of John's protests to the contrary, she affirms that John continues to yearn for her. Thus confronted, John admits to thinking of her "softly from time to time. But," he insists, "I will cut off my hand before I ever reach for you again" (p. 241). Suddenly the words "going up to Jesus" are heard from below and Betty sits up, wailing. Parris, the Putnams, Rebecca Nurse, and Giles Corey quickly enter the room. Rebecca is presented as a saintly old woman; Giles is eighty-three, and "canny" (p. 242). An argument develops between John and Parris in which the latter accuses the preacher of too much love for money, hellfire sermons, and the rights of authority. In fact, Proctor explains that it is these faults of Parris that have kept many, including Proctor himself, from attending church recently. There is also an altercation between John and Mr. Putnam over the latter's land claims. Hale enters just as John is leaving. Questioned by Hale, Abigail confesses that Tituba forced her to drink chicken blood. Tituba admits to conjuring, but also implicates others in Salem. Abigail joins with the slave in this strategy, as do the other frightened girls, and the act ends with the girls "crying out" against various people.

Act Two takes place eight days later in the "common room of Proctor's house." A strain is evident between John and Elizabeth Proctor. Elizabeth urges John to go to court and reveal that

Abigail told him that there was no conjuring in the woods.
When John says there were no witnesses to Abigail's statement,
Elizabeth traps her husband in a lie, for he had previously denied being alone with the girl. Elizabeth suspects John of still
lusting after Abigail, while John accuses his wife of being unfor-
giving. When Mary returns from Salem, she gives Elizabeth a
doll she made that day at court. The girl reports that if a
prisoner confesses to witchcraft he is in no danger of being
hanged. John, unimpressed by the "leniency" of the court, hotly
forbids Mary to return to Salem. Mary defends herself by asserting that she saved Eliazbeth's life when the latter was accused
of sorcery. Elizabeth is convinced that Abigail wants her dead.
Hale enters, then, and probes into the spiritual life of the Proctors. He has noticed, in going through the church records, that
John does not often appear at services. When John attempts to
shift the blame to Parris, Hale requests that John recite the
Commandments. John obliges—but omits the sin of adultery.
Hale grows increasingly disturbed about the Proctors. Suddenly
Giles appears and informs the Proctors that Rebecca and Mrs.
Corey have both been arrested. Court officers arrive on the scene
and, in a search of the house, discover the doll. Since the doll has
a needle in it, Elizabeth is arrested as a witch, for that evening
Abigail was stabbed with a needle. There is a moment of hope
when Mary admits to having made the doll herself and that
Abigail saw her stick the needle in it when she was finished.
Nevertheless, the officers insist on removing Elizabeth to jail.
Hale exits affirming his faith in the trials, claiming that some
secret sin "may have drawn from heaven such thundering wrath
upon you all" (p. 283). Proctor, who "has been reached by
Hale's words" (p. 283), informs Mary that she must tell the
truth in court. When Mary reminds John that Abigail will accuse him of "lechery," he declares that his wife will not die for
him:

    Now Hell and Heaven grapple on our backs, and all our

old pretense is ripped away. . . . It is a providence, and no great change; we are only what we always were, but naked now. *He walks as though toward a great horror, facing the open sky.* Aye, naked! And the wind, God's icy wind, will blow! (p. 284)

Act Three, which unfolds in the "vestry room of the Salem meeting house," occurs at some point during the following summer. Deputy-Governor Danforth, who has condemned seventy-two people to be hanged, receives a deposition from John signed by Mary Warren and testifying that she saw no evil spirits. In addition, John has secured a list of names of people in Salem who protest the trials. Although Danforth is shaken, he remains unconvinced, for he suspects John of seeking to undermine the court. The Deputy-Governor grows more suspicious when John, even after Danforth agrees to drop charges against the pregnant Elizabeth for a year, refuses to destroy the deposition. John, however, asserts that he is merely fighting for others, such as Giles, who has also been arrested. Danforth is again shaken in his resolve when the girls, under questioning, own to having danced in the woods. When Abigail refuses to admit anything more, though, John feels constrained to confess "lechery" with her. To test the validity of John's confession, Danforth sends for Elizabeth. The Deputy-Governor reasons that Mrs. Proctor, being a good woman, would not tell a lie, even to save her husband's life. Danforth is mistaken about Elizabeth, however, for she does lie to protect John. Danforth thus feels vindicated, but Hale, who is no longer certain about the rightness of the trials, defends John. To distract the court, Abigail suddenly starts screaming. Mary, caught up by her friend's fakery, accuses John of being "the Devil's man" (p. 310). John is immediately arrested, and Hale quits the court.

The concluding act takes place in the fall of 1692 in a "cell in Salem jail." It is reported that Abigail has stolen Parris's money and has disappeared. Although rebellion threatens Salem, Dan-

forth is determined to continue the trials. Hale, horrified by the
excesses of the trials, pleads with Elizabeth to get John to confess, declaring that it would be better for John to lie than to
hang—a line of persuasion that Elizabeth brands the "Devil's
argument" (p. 310). When Elizabeth is alone with John, she
informs him that Giles is dead. John, feeling unsuited for the
heroic role, is confused about what he should do. Elizabeth
wants John alive, but she says that whatever he does, she believes him to be a good man now. Elizabeth even admits to having prompted his affair with Abigail by being a cold wife to him.
John, however, refuses to believe in his goodness. "Nothing's
spoiled," he says, "by giving them this lie that were not rotten
long before" (p. 322). John, who wants his life too, finally decides to confess. When Danforth demands John's signature to
his confession, however, something within John rebels: "How
may I live without my name? I have given you my soul; leave
me my name!" (p. 328). Furiously, John destroys the confession. As he is removed for execution, John declares:

> now I do think I see some shred of goodness in John
> Proctor. Not enough to weave a banner with, but white
> enough to keep it from such dogs. . . . Show honor now,
> show a stony heart and sink them with it! (p. 328)

After John's exit, Hale says: "Shall the dust praise him? Shall
the worms declare his truth?" To which Elizabeth replies: "He
have his goodness now. God forbid I take it from him!" (p. 329).
    Reviewers were in disagreement whether the opening act, or
Overture, was too slow or too fast. My summary of Act One
should suggest an answer to this critical problem. Abigail, it was
noted, enters on the first page of dialogue; by the next page, an
atmosphere of witchcraft and perverted sexuality is suggested;
and by the third page, it is related that Abigail was discharged
by Elizabeth and that her name has been "soiled." This would
seem to be economical and subtle foreshadowing and exposition.

True, John, who is the protagonist, does not enter until the eighth page of dialogue; but once he does enter, the future development of the play begins to outline itself. Moreover, according to Lajos Egri, there are various ways of determining the point of attack. "A play might start at a point where at least one character has reached a turning point in his life"; if so, the first page of *The Crucible* qualifies because Parris has clearly "reached a turning point." "A play might start exactly at the point where a conflict will lead up to a crisis"; if this is true, the first page again qualifies, since the argument between Parris and Abigail prepares the reader for future complications. "A good point of attack is where something vital is at stake at the very beginning of the play"; on the first page, Betty's life is in danger, and on the second page, Parris's job is at stake. However, if the point of attack be reserved for the protagonist, for the moment when John is caught up in the conflict, then the attack occurs on the ninth page, in the scene between Abigail and John when their past and present relations are disclosed, and a question is raised concerning their future relations. But the major dramatic question, which I will discuss in its complexity below, is posed in the person of Parris from the very start of the play: How should a man act in the face of evil? (Parris's "reply" seems to be that one should protect himself at any cost.) Since there are about twenty-five pages of dialogue in Act One, it is safe to say that the point of attack (however defined) occurs before one-third of the act is completed. Even if the attack arrives relatively late (ninth page), the situation is not comparable to the first act of *All My Sons*, for here Miller has provided sufficient conflict from the opening curtain. By the seventh page of dialogue, the situation of the frightened girls begins to assume shape. Nine characters (eight, if we omit Betty, who does not engage in dialogue) appear prior to John's entrance; however, they are introduced slowly, they are each, depending on their relative importance in the action, given time to establish themselves, and the dramatic line, as I have tried to show, is kept sufficiently clear and relevant. Much more is going on here, for Miller is skillfully creating a dense social context within which John Proctor will work out his fate. It would seem, then, that Act One is more than a mere introduction to the action; that the point of attack occurs immediately or, at the most, fairly early; that, from the standpoint of conflict, the act is moderately paced, and, finally, that the exposition is clear and direct.

In terms of sustained conflict, Acts Two and Three are the most dramatic. These middle acts focus on thrust and counter-thrust, and the tension is generally high. The outcome is never certain until John is arrested at the conclusion to Act Three, and even here there is a question raised—hence continuing suspense—because the reader is not certain whether John will confess or die. Gerald Weales has criticized the turning point, which he calls "romantic" and "sentimental," because it hinges on Elizabeth's lie to save her husband, and he compares the plot in this respect to the hidden-letter revelation in *All My Sons*, adding that this device is removed from the main line of motivation in the play represented by John's inner torment of conscience. There is, of course, no scientific test to prove that Miller's scene is not "romantic" or "sentimental"; but one might point out that the comparison to *All My Sons* is not in order. In the earlier play, the letter was a complete surprise, and, moreover, a character whom the audience had never seen untied the knot for Miller. In *The Crucible*, as will be shown in detail below, Elizabeth prepares the reader for her behavior at the turning point, and, what is perhaps more important, her action is not divorced from the main line of motivation in the play, for her response is part of the thematic thrust of the play, one "answer" to the question: How should a man—or woman—act in the face of evil?

In Act Four, the thematic question is very largely focused upon a single issue: Will John Proctor confess to save his neck —or will he die? Tension grows out of John's struggle with his conscience. Dialogue, it should be noted, is used effectively to augment tension through the constant references to the dawn, which spells execution, for there are five such references within thirteen pages. The crisis occurs about two and a half pages before the final curtain:

> Proctor has just finished signing when Danforth reaches for the paper. But Proctor snatches it up, and now a wild terror is rising in him, and a boundless anger. (p. 327)

At this point, we do not know whether Proctor will return the confession or die, but we sense that the decisive moment has at last arrived. The climax comes about a page and a half later when John "tears the paper and crumbles it" (p. 328). Kenneth Tynan has called the last scene "old melodrama." Admittedly, John's speeches are somewhat stagy at the end. As I have tried to suggest in the description of Act Four, however, the action develops to its crisis and climax through a series of smooth transitions. John's growth is consistent and credible. It is a gross misreading of the play to view it in terms of the "wholly right" and the "wholly wrong"—that is, in melodramatic terms—for an analysis of theme will make clear that Crucible is more complex than critics have generally allowed. Miller himself has distorted this feature of his play. In the "Introduction," he claims that the characters are black in Crucible because the "historical facts . . . were immutable," and he adds that if he were to write it again he would make them even more black (pp. 42-43).

It might be objected that John, being the protagonist, is absent from the scene too much of the time. In fact, John is absent on about twenty-eight pages out of the roughly ninety-three pages of dialogue—in short, John is not "there" during one-third of the play. Abigail, who is the antagonist, does not appear at all in the second and fourth acts. Perhaps adherence to his sources imposed certain restrictions on Miller's creative imagination. However, in view of the fact that Crucible has a multi-focused theme, John's absence from the scene for certain periods would not appear to be a serious matter. The mere report of Abigail's disappearance in Act Four, on the other hand, seems like a weak device. One would not wish to imply that Miller has missed an obligatory scene here; yet it is no doubt true that the reader misses a confrontation between John and Abigail in the last act. True, the struggle in Act Three is highly effective: John's confession of "lechery" is a strong thrust, and Abigail's ability to sway Mary against John is a powerful counter-thrust. Nevertheless, one feels a gap in Act Four. One looks for a scene to balance the one in the "Overture"—a scene, for example, in which Abigail seemingly triumphs over John ("seemingly," because not "spiritually") and, since nobody would believe John anyway, informs him herself of her plans to disappear, for the concrete is preferable to the abstract report.

Perhaps it was some sense of a lack in the structure of the play that prompted Miller to add a new scene between John and Abigail in a later production of *Crucible*. The printed version of the new scene appeared in *Theatre Arts* in October 1953. Although the scene is said to have been added to Act Two, it appears in *Theatre Arts* in isolation after the first act curtain. It is a short scene and, in my opinion, it adds nothing vitally significant to the original version; it merely makes explicit what was fairly obvious from Abigail's actions in the original treatment. In addition, the new scene is marred by a too overt straining after irony. When Miller brought out the *Collected Plays* four years later, the new scene was not in evidence.

The main characters in *Crucible*, contrary to some critical reports, are far from flat. John Proctor is described as a "farmer in his middle thirties" (p. 238), "powerful of body" (p. 239). In his first scene, John reveals himself as a man with a strong personality: "Abigail has stood as though on tiptoe, absorbing his presence, wide-eyed," while the other girl is "strangely titillated" (p. 239). That Abigail is willing to murder in order to possess John invests this farmer with a sense of importance. That John lusted with the girl in the past—against the law of

God and Salem—reveals a certain daring in the man. That John has the will power to resist Abigail now, even while part of him still desires her, shows determination. Repeatedly, John displays his dislike of authoritarianism.

In Act Two, John makes a determined effort to please Elizabeth. His kisses her perfunctorily; he lies in saying that her cooking is well-seasoned (perhaps a kind of irony on the lack of spice in Elizabeth?). John seems motivated by guilt feelings in this scene. When Elizabeth urges him to go to court and expose Abigail, he is afraid that his relations with the girl will be brought to light. The question of whether the court will believe him (p. 262 and p. 275) would seem of secondary importance. The cardinal point is that John must struggle against his own fear. Miller attempts to integrate the "personal" and the "social" in a number of ways. "I cannot speak but I am doubted," says John, ". . . as though I come into a court when I come into this house!" (p. 265). Although John lies to Elizabeth about being alone with Abigail in Parris's house (p. 264), he persists in defending his honesty (p. 265).

John continues to struggle, throughout Act Three, against both his inner contradictions and his outer antagonists. He reveals his resourcefulness in securing a deposition. He shows his persistence in extracting a confession from Mary. When the charge against Elizabeth is suspended, John does not falter—he concentrates his attack on the court for the sake of others. And when Abigail seems to be winning the struggle, John makes public confession of his "lechery."

In Act Four, John "is another man, bearded, filthy, his eyes misty as though webs had overgrown them" (p. 320). The physical transformation signals an inner change in John. "I have been thinking," he tells Elizabeth, "I would confess to them" (p. 322). After a few months in jail contemplating his death a change of appearance and attitude on John's part is credible. John defends himself by saying: "Spite only keeps me silent" (p. 323); "I want my life" (p. 324). However, John has not overcome his inner conflict; he hesitates to implicate others (p. 326); he balks at signing the confession (p. 327). Gradually, John moves to a position of final defiance of the court: "I have three children—how may I teach them to walk like men . . . and I sold my friends?" (p. 327).

The foregoing shows clearly that John is rich in traits; that there is continuous development of his character; and that there is adequate preparation for his revelation in the last act.

No critic, as far as I know, has questioned John Proctor's status as a "tragic hero." The controversy over the "common man" versus the "traditional hero" (usually Aristotelian), occasioned by the fate of Willy Loman, is absent from discussions of *Crucible*. Miller would seem to have provided Proctor with all the heroic attributes dear to the heart of "traditionalists." Miller himself says: "In *The Crucible* . . . the characters were special people who could give voice to the things that were inside them. . . . These people knew what was happening to them" (*Theatre Arts*, October 1953). Whether this increase in articulateness makes *Crucible* a more powerful dramatic piece than *Death of a Salesman* is arguable.

Dialogue, it should be noted, fails to illuminate John's past. Is this lack of background a serious failing in *Crucible?* In *All My Sons*, lack of adequate character exposition impaired credibility; in *Salesman*, the revelation of Willy's past had a direct bearing on the present line of development. In *Crucible*, however, the past would not seem to be pertinent. Each play should be approached on its own merits. *Crucible* focuses on a specific situation, and the reader possesses all the necessary facts for believing in that situation. Nor should one conclude that, since John's final speeches sound too theatrical, the language in the play is not adequate. The various summaries presented in this chapter should indicate that preparation, especially foreshadowing of character development, is expertly handled. Miller, in a very subtle manner, uses key words to knit together the texture of action and theme. Note, for example, the recurrent use of the word "soft." In Act One, John tells Abigail: "Abby, I may think of you *softly* from time to time. . . ." (p. 241, italics mine); in Act Two, Hale tells John: "there is a *softness* in your record, sir, a *softness*" (p. 273, italics mine). Dialogue, moreover, suggests that behind John's denunciation of Parris lies a guilty conscience. Hale says that John has missed church services a good deal in the past seventeen months (p. 252); since Abigail has been removed from Proctor's house for the past seven months (p. 232), the inference is that the real reason for John's backsliding has not been expressed.

Miller is even more sparing than usual in his physical description of Elizabeth; that is, not one word is uttered about her appearance. Nor, as was the case with John, is anything conveyed about her background. Nevertheless, Elizabeth has many traits and she grows throughout the play. She is sensitive: "It hurt my heart to strip her, poor rabbit" (p. 262); here, of course, Elizabeth is a foil to the murderous Abigail. Elizabeth betrays a weakness in asserting herself against Mary Warren, a weakness which John brands a "fault" (p. 263). She is also proud (p. 273), slow to forgive (p. 265), and suspicious (p. 265). Frequently, Elizabeth—who is "cold" (p. 323)—fails in charity (p. 265). But she will lie for a loved one (p. 307), and, since she learns humility (p. 323), she is capable of change. Elizabeth's dominant motive is her yearning for John's undivided love. In Act Two, for instance, behind Elizabeth's self-righteous and intolerant posture, there is love for John. She proves this love in Act Three when she lies to save John's life. Elizabeth continues to grow in the last act. "Her wrists," says Miller, "are linked by heavy chain. . . . Her clothes are dirty; her face is pale and gaunt" (p. 319). The trials have worked their effect on Elizabeth, too. Danforth, uncomprehending, sees in her "dry eyes" the "proof of [her] unnatural life" (p. 320). Alone with her husband, however, Elizabeth says:

I have read my heart this three month John. . . . I have

sins of my own to count. It need a cold wife to prompt lechery. (p. 323)

John, I counted myself so plain, so poorly made, no honest love could come to me! Suspicion kissed you when I did; I never knew how I should say my love. It were a cold house I kept. (p. 323)

Since Elizabeth remains in character, her development in Act Four, as was the case with John, is logical and believable.

Abigail is much less complex and interesting than either John or Elizabeth. She is described as "seventeen . . . a strikingly beautiful girl, an orphan, with an endless capacity for dissembling" (p. 230). Dialogue fails to disclose anything about Abigail's past. In the course of the play, however, she reveals several traits: she is supersensitive (p. 238), sexually passionate (p. 240), and mentally alert (p. 259); she is commanding (p. 238) and vain (p. 305); she is a thief (pp. 315-316); and throughout the play, she makes painfully evident that she is capable of murder. Abigail's dominant motive is to destroy Elizabeth and sleep with John. Abigail remains in character; but she does not grow.

The minor characters, with the exception of Hale, are flat and static. There is a question of Miller's economy here, and Miller himself was not unaware of the problem ("Introduction," p. 42). In *All My Sons*, Miller seemed to have employed more characters than he needed for the furtherance of either action or theme. In *The Crucible*, in spite of the fact that there are at least twenty-one characters, the problem does not seem acute, for as was pointed out in the discussion of structure, Miller managed to keep the developing action in thematic focus. If the numerous characters, such as, Marshall Herrick or Ezekiel Cheever, contribute very little, if anything, to action or theme, it is also true that they do nothing to impede or becloud action and theme. Some readers might find many of these secondary figures mere "scenery"; whether Miller might have profitably eliminated them entirely is an interesting, but hardly a burning, technical question.

Although the characters will be discussed again in the following section, it should be noted here that all the leading ones represent various shadings on a thematic spectrum. John wavers between principle and compromise, and chooses, finally, principle; Elizabeth opts for John's "goodness," no matter what he finally chooses; Abigail is completely self-seeking; so is Parris; Rebecca is a witness to principle above compromise or deceit; Danforth is similarly unyielding about the inviolability of principle; while Hale, who alone among the minor characters grows, would abandon principle for the sake of life. This schematic neatness suggests that *Crucible* is not to be evaluated by a narrow adherence to a realistic or naturalistic norm. In the *Theatre Arts* issue last cited, Miller says: "*The Crucible* is not more realistic but more theatrical than *Death of a Salesman*." Yet it would be a serious error to leap to the other extreme and dismiss Miller's play as a mere oversimplified morality play. Miller himself, as I have suggested, invites the latter approach, but it is entirely possible that the playwright, no less than his hostile critics, has missed the very real thematic complexity that *is* in *The Crucible*.

Certainly Eric Bentley has missed this complexity, for—dubbing Miller "the playwright of American liberalism"—he finds in *Crucible* "a conflict between the wholly guilty and the wholly innocent." Bentley agrees that, "The guilty men are as black with guilt as Mr. Miller says," but adds, "What we must ask is whether the innocent are as innocent." (That, as Bentley says, the "guilty" are as "black" as Miller claims seems like a rather curious statement; presumably Bentley intends the "historically guilty"—though one never knows for certain in this article, since Bentley hops in and out of Salem, contemporary events, Miller's essays, and *The Crucible*, without leaving a discernible trail.) Robert Warshow (highly praised by Bentley —perhaps because Warshow finds Miller's plays "neat" but

"empty") and David Levine, among others, are disturbed because Miller has falsified history—Levine adding that the "error" is also an "aesthetic" one.

Let us dispose of the historical argument, at least for the
moment, by agreeing that Miller might have written an enjoy-
able and complex play had he given more attention to religious
and philosophical factors that were important to Salem in 1692.
In fact, however, Miller wrote *this* play—*The Crucible*—and
regardless of his "intentions," his historical "errors," or his
faulty contemporary parallel, the task for the critic is whether
the play that *is*, is sufficiently complex and "aesthetic" on its
own terms. One might read the play, as many critics have done,
as an attack on enforced conformity; in my opinion, however,
such a reading is narrow and superficial, and misses the deeper
thrust of the play. Warshow asks: "But if Mr. Miller isn't saying anything about the Salem trials, and can't be caught saying
anything about anything else [read McCarthy], what did the
audience think he was saying?" What follows is an attempt to
discover what Miller is "saying" in *The Crucible*.

As has been said, the thematic question projected by the action of the play would seem to be: How should a man act in
the face of evil? It has also been suggested that the individual
"replies" to the question are represented by the various significant actors in the drama. Abigail may be omitted from serious
consideration here; although she is vital to the plot she contributes little or nothing to the theme. Similarly, the other girls
may be placed to one side here, and the same stricture applies
to Parris and the Putnams; no noble aims seem to motivate
them. (I will return to these characters later, however, in discussing the motives for the trials.) All the significant responses
to the action are conveyed by six principal characters.

Danforth, it is important to remember, is motivated by the
fact that he is an orthodox Puritan who fully believes in the
existence of evil spirits (p. 291). As the symbol of authority,
Danforth assumes exact knowledge of "God's law" (p. 318),

and, taking a rigid stance on the letter of that law, he pursues the logic of what he conceives the facts to be to their inevitable end (p. 297). Danforth's mind, the mind of a lawyer, makes sharp, rational distinctions (p. 293): for him, a principle is sacred, and he would not hesitate, since he sees his way clearly, to sacrifice all human life for a single principle (p. 318). Like many God-surrogates, Danforth seems to be a proud man; but behind his stiff posture there now and then lurks the fear, never wholly embraced or articulated, that he might be in serious error (p. 301). After Danforth has sentenced nearly one hundred men and women to be hanged, he has a *personal* stake in the justice of the trials; he is almost coerced into assuming an "either-or" view of good and evil (p. 293), for to admit the unknowable, the ambiguous, the irrational, into experience would be to expose "God" [read Danforth and Salem law] to the confusion and uncertainty of a world suddenly turned upside down by inexplicable events.

Hale might be considered as a foil to Danforth. He begins as fully confident of his moral position as the Deputy-Governor, for in his books, Hale has evil neatly "caught, defined, and calculated" (p. 253). Life, however, refutes the books; and Hale, more sensitive than Danforth, more comprehending, permits doubt to enter, like a corrosive chemical, into his soul (pp. 275, 292). As a result, Hale no longer is convinced that he is privy to the decrees of the most high; on the contrary, asserting that God's will is often in darkness, he assumes the radical ambiguity of moral questions (p. 320). Where Danforth declares that he would "hang ten thousand that dared to rise against the law" (p. 318), Hale avers: "life is God's most precious gift; no principle . . . may justify the taking of it" (p. 320).

Rebecca Nurse resembles the very man who condemns her to be hanged. Like Danforth, she would not sacrifice a principle even if it should cost her her life (p. 325). Like Danforth, she appears to have no sense of guilt; she tells John: "Let you fear nothing! Another judgment waits us all!" (p. 328). Like Danforth, Rebecca sees little of life's complexity (are there no "real life" counterparts to Danforth and Rebecca?); she is merely "astonished" at John's lie to save his life (p. 325).

Giles Corey's position on the thematic spectrum suggests a stance somewhere between the extremes of "nobility" (represented by those who take morals seriously) and "ignobility" (Parris, say, or the Putnams). Although Giles fights against the evil of the trials, he dies—not for the sake of an abstract principle of right—but in such a way as to insure that his property will go to his sons (p. 322).

Elizabeth Proctor is more complex than Danforth, Hale, Giles, and Rebecca. Elizabeth, like Hale, is willing to sacrifice an abstraction when it seems, to her, expedient to do so; but, unlike Hale, she does not "rationalize" her argument; "subjective," not "objective" arguments dictate her actions. In Act Two, Elizabeth sacrifices logic to her pride; she tells Hale that she believes in the Gospels (and the Gospels affirm the existence of witches); but she adds that if Hale thinks that she could "do only good work in the world, and yet be secretly bound to Satan, then I must tell you, sir, I do not believe it" (p. 276). In Act Three, Elizabeth sacrifices a principle to save her husband's life; her motive here is not pride, as it was above, but love. In Act Four, she refuses to answer John's question whether she would lie to save her own life; John believes that she would not lie (p. 324). On the basis of her record, how can John—or the reader—be certain? Elizabeth says she wants John alive (p. 322)—which scarcely allows John much choice in the matter. No longer self-righteous, Elizabeth stresses her own frailty (p. 323); repeatedly she says: "I cannot judge you, John" (p. 322, p. 323, and twice on p. 324); and she adds: "Whatever you will do, it is a good man does it" (p. 323). This is important. Elizabeth seems to be saying that a man may lie and be "good"—or, equally, a man may refuse to lie and be "good." How can this be "true"? It would seem idle to argue the matter philosophically or semantically; for instance, one might say that "good" is a vague term, or that Elizabeth means that John has not confessed until now, and regardless of what he does later, that (as Elizabeth tells John): "speak goodness in you" (p. 323). However, it would seem more rewarding, for the critic if not the philosopher, to ask: What has Elizabeth revealed about herself that permits her to hold such a belief? Early in Act Four, when Hale suggests that Elizabeth persuade John to lie in order to save himself, she says: "I think that be the Devil's argument" (p. 320); but when faced by John, she says, in effect, that a man might use the "Devil's argument" and still be a "good" man. Elizabeth is not inconsistent here; we have seen that she has previously sacrificed principle for personal ends; we have also seen that she has reached a stage in her growth toward humility when she is, at least for the moment, more concerned with the "beam in her own eye."

John Proctor's response to events is, of course, the most complicated one in the play; moreover, his role as protagonist would appear to lend his position more validity than that of the other characters. Since John's development has been traced above, little need be added here. It is worth stressing, however, that John thought he was "good" in Act Two (p. 265); but as it developed, John was self-deceived—in his heart, he still lusted after Abigail (p. 241). At the end of the play, John again believes in his "goodness" (p. 328); but Hale, in effect, says that John is once again self-deceived: "It is pride, it is vanity" (p. 329).

Who is right? I repeat: *The Crucible* would not seem to be the simple, didactic, polemical play that most critics, including Miller himself perhaps, would have us believe. Although the characters, with the exception of John, Elizabeth, and possibly Hale, are constructed along relatively simple lines, the multiple points of view are complex and well-orchestrated. John's role in the play, then, would seem to be limited, and the position he takes qualified, by the stance of the other characters. *The Crucible* cannot be reduced to a single statement, or thesis, without doing violence to the total impression conveyed by the play. In *All My Sons*, it was otherwise; but John's death "proves" nothing—Hale is not made to "see the light" (as, say, Chris Keller was illuminated), Danforth does not kill himself (as Joe Keller was made to do). At the end of the drama, the "meaning" of the play is focused from four different angles: Danforth considers John's death a just punishment: "Who weeps for these, weeps for corruption!" (p. 328); Hale views John's death as meaningless: "What profit him to bleed?" (p. 329); John's view has already been quoted (p. 328)—in the last analysis John belongs with those who refuse to sacrifice a principle; while Elizabeth says: "He have his goodness now. God forbid I take it from him!" (p. 329). Since Elizabeth's line is the final one of the play, the critic may not automatically assume that it is the only "right" one; after all, *had John lied Elizabeth would have said the same thing*. The play is complex because John *is* a "good" man; so is Hale; so is Giles; Elizabeth and Rebecca are "good" too—for only "good" people do battle with evil. Even Danforth is not black—given his cast of mind and the times, one can, at least, understand his position (those who call him "wholly guilty" would seem to be doing the play an injustice through oversimplification). "In my play," says Miller, "Danforth seems about to conceive of the truth, and surely there is a disposition in him at least to listen to arguments that go counter to the line of the prosecution. There is no such swerving in the record" ("Introduction," p. 43). The text supports Miller's statement. At the end of Act Three, however, when John accuses Danforth of knowing that the trials are a fraud, there is no evidence in the text to prove John right. Similarly, in the last act, when Danforth asserts that he "will not deal in lies" (p. 328), there is no data in the play itself which will refute him. In regard to the ending of the third act, one suspects (which was the case in the Requiem of *Salesman*) that Miller has sacrificed a fine regard for the facts in his play for the sake of an effective curtain. The sharpest conflict in the play, ideologically, might very well be between Hale's counsel of compromise and John's inflexibility. And who is wise enough to dogmatize upon the matter once and for all?

Granting, it might be objected, that *Crucible* contains more variety than is usually allowed for it, is it not true that it remains a bit too simple? For some readers, the neatness of the thematic spectrum is perhaps an argument against the play's complexity, and for those who demand shading, not among multiple points of view but in each individual character, Miller's play is unsatisfactory. The same readers may also feel that Proctor's infidelity is not enough of a complication, that it is too flimsy a foundation on which to erect the structure of *Crucible*. The crucial question, however, is: Does Miller succeed in fusing the "personal" and the "social"? A close reading of the play would suggest that he does. A flaw in Proctor's marriage allows the trials to materialize; no act—even the most intimate of sexual relations—would seem isolated from the "social." Elizabeth admits to being "cold"; but it is not due to being "puritanical," as some critics would have it, or to "lack of love"; she says (as I have quoted previously): "John, I counted myself so plain, so poorly made, no honest love could come to me! . . . I never knew how I should say my love" (p. 323). John asks: "Is the accuser always holy now?" (p. 281). This has both a "personal" and a "social" reference; "personal" because Elizabeth accuses John of evil and she is not "holy" (although she admits her faults later), while John himself learns that he is not as "holy" as he had thought; "social" because, to take but one instance, Abigail and the girls are not "holy" but they accuse others. This much is fairly obvious. As was also quoted above, Miller *intended* to focus on "that guilt residing in Salem which the hysteria merely unleashed" ("Introduction," p. 42). Is it necessary that the guilt be of a single kind? Is it not possible—indeed probable—that various kinds of

guilt may come to focus upon a single "social" situation? Of
course, Elizabeth admits to keeping a "cold house" (p. 323);
and Salem is a "cold" community; and the activity of the girls
in the woods suggests sexual repression—but this is far from
being the entire explanation of events. And, as Miller *drama-
tizes* his material, guilt is not the sole motive for the trials. Nor
would it seem either necessary or desirable that it should be in
order to link the "personal" to the "social." Some critics want
a single explanation for the "enemy"; but certainly the interest
of the play, for a mature reader, is that the "enemy" assumes
many shapes and refuses to be reduced to a single motivation.
Mrs. Putnam is filled with hate because she lost seven babies at
birth; Mr. Putnam wants land; Parris wants to protect his job;
Tituba wants to save her neck; Abigail wants John—and so it
goes. If it be objected that few of these characters seem
genuinely convinced of witchcraft, that would seem to be more
of an historical than an aesthetic question. Miller, it must be
owned, exposed himself to such criticism by identifying his play
with a specific period. It is certainly arguable whether we get,
as Miller says we do, the "essential nature" of the Salem trials;
but no matter—what we do get is an extremely effective drama.
Yet, even from the merely "historical" standpoint, Miller has
complicated his action; for example, and this is to the modern
taste, Betty appears to be suffering from some kind of self-
damaging guilt complex brought about from the previous
night's outing in the woods; but there is a nice question how
much Abigail and the girls really believe in witchcraft. Although
Abigail tells Parris (p. 231) and John (p. 240) that it was just
a "sport," she *did* drink chicken blood as a charm to kill Elizabeth (p. 238), which suggests that Miller has mixed various
kinds of motives to propel his action.

Intrinsically, *The Crucible* is complex, coherent, and convincing; that is, it succeeds *as a play* on its own premises and
merits. Although one might hesitate to agree that *The Crucible*
is superior to *Death of a Salesman*—it seems to lack the sen-

suousness, the imaginative and technical brilliance, even the warm humanity, of the earlier play—still it remains one of Miller's best plays and one of the most impressive achievements of the American theater.

CHAPTER FOUR

A Memory of Two Mondays

A *Memory of Two Mondays* (1955) is a long one-act play. In his introduction to the original edition of the play in 1955, Miller said: "My ambition is to write shorter and shorter plays. It is harder to hit a target with one bullet—perhaps that is why." Whether Miller has "hit a target" in A *Memory of Two Mondays* is, of course, precisely the critical question.

The play is concerned with a group of auto-parts workers in a New York City warehouse in the Thirties:

> The two basic structures are the long packing table which curves upstage at the left, and the factory-type windows which reach from floor to ceiling and are encrusted with the hard dirt of years. These windows are the background and seem to surround the entire stage.
>
> . . . .
>
> The nature of the work is simple. The men take orders off the hook, go out into the bin-lined alleys, fill the orders, bring the merchandise back to the table, where Kenneth packs and addresses everything. The desk is used by Gus and/or Tom Kelly to figure postage or express rates on, to eat on, to lean on, or to hide things in. It is just home base generally.
>
> A warning: The place must seem dirty and unmanageably chaotic, but since it is seen in this play with two

separate visions it is also romantic. It is a little world, a home to which, unbelievably perhaps, these people like to come every Monday morning, despite what they say. (pp. 332-333)

Miller's reference to "two separate visions" needs underlining. In the introduction noted above, Miller defines the play as "abstract realism in form." By this, Miller presumably intends that his play alternates between a presentational, lyrical, or expressionistic form and a representational, or realistic, mode of imitation. A word on this alternation is perhaps in order here before the matter is discussed in more detail below. A *Memory of Two Mondays* is largely in the representational mode; it is realistic in action and dialogue from pages 333 to 356; there is then a transition between the two Mondays of the play in what is mainly a presentational mode (there is non-realistic stage lighting and the characters speak in soliloquy and free verse) which covers two pages; the second Monday is also rendered in a realistic form from pages 359 to 370; there is one switch to the presentational mode, pages 370 to 371; and from then on the play continues to the final curtain—pages 372 to 376—in the predominant realistic style.

The first Monday occurs in summer. The transition between the Mondays moves in time through autumn to a winter day. How much time has elapsed, however, is not definitely stated. At the start of the play Bert, the protagonist, says that he will leave the place in a year (p. 334), and since the end of the play enacts his leaving, probably a little less than a year passes in the course of the play.

It is not easy to summarize the action in this long one-act play. Miller himself suggests the reason when he says:

A *Memory of Two Mondays* has a story but not a plot, because the life it reflects appears to me to strip people of alternatives and will beyond a close and tight pe-

riphery in which they may exercise a meager choice.
("Introduction," p. 50)

Miller's remarks might be misleading by suggesting that his
play lacks conscious artistry; although A *Memory of Two Mondays* has, in the conventional sense, no plot, this is not to say
that it has no pattern of development, no increment of tension,
and no unifying elements.

On the first Monday of the play, Bert is introduced as an
eighteen-year-old boy who is reading *War and Peace* on the
subway and who, after he has earned enough money to enter
college, will leave the warehouse in a year. If A *Memory* were
fiction, Bert might be described as the "central observer." True,
Bert does not influence the action—what "action" there is,
since there is no plot—but he does appear to be the hub around
which the story revolves. There is a contrast here between the
dynamic and the static—between Bert who is transitory and
free and the group who are permanent and trapped. Miller
introduces his workers slowly as they enter the warehouse to
work.

Ray, the manager, is worried because the owner, Mr. Eagle,
is coming. Jim, seventy-five, enters, half-drunk. Gus, sixty-eight,
chases the spinster Agnes into the toilet, beseeching her to visit
Atlantic City with him, in the same breath informing the
woman that his wife is dying. Gus and Jim had been drinking
together all weekend, and Gus had not even bothered to phone
his wife. He does so now, however, but he hangs up when she
fails to understand him immediately. Kenneth, twenty-six, arrives; he is an Irishman and fond of poetry, and he seems to
be the one character capable of understanding Bert. Next to
appear is Larry. He is married, but he informs the girl, Patricia,
that he bought a new Auburn and that he would like to drive
her home after work.

Certain patterns gradually establish themselves. Gus breaks
the monotony of the work by chasing Agnes and Patricia

around the room. Ken, whose sensitivity is apparent, complains of the dust and the dirt. Frank, the driver, comes and goes. People file in and out of the single toilet. In short, the rhythm of the work is caught and the private lives of the workers are partially defined through their response to the work routine.

The excitement for the morning is to be provided by Tom Kelly. Tom, who is almost fifty, arrives "stiff," and the task for his friends will be to keep his condition secret from Mr. Eagle. While this problem is discussed, Kenneth and Larry complain about the deadening routine of the warehouse, and Kenneth asks why the windows cannot be clean. Gus, who is hardened to it all, tells the Irishman to be quiet. Suddenly it is announced that Eagle has arrived, and Tom is propped rigidly at his desk, a pencil is jammed into his lifeless hand, and the strategy is for all to act unconcerned. While Eagle passes through the room, Tom abruptly starts from his alcoholic haze and appears to sober. As Eagle departs, the workers, believing that their ruse has succeeded, are delighted; but a moment later, Ray enters and announces that Eagle wants to see Tom, and the happiness that had filled the room quickly disappears. Ray is certain that Tom will be fired; Gus threatens to quit. While they are waiting for the result of Tom's interview with Eagle, the phone rings and Gus is informed that his wife is dead. Tom, beaming happily, returns then and says that Eagle has given him one more chance. Ray calls the workers to their tasks—and all scatter.

The first Monday is drawing to its close. The stage is empty save for Bert, Kenneth, and Tom. Says Kenneth (and the transition begins here):

> Bert? How would you feel about washing these windows . . . once and for all? Let a little of God's light in the place? (pp. 356-357)

Bert agrees:

Let's do a little every day; couple of months it'll all be clean! (p. 357)

Both men set to work on the windows, and dialogue drifts into verse form:

It'll be nice [says Kenneth] to watch the seasons pass.
That pretty up there now, a real summer sky
And a little white cloud goin' over?
I can just see autumn comin' in
And the leaves falling on the gray days.
You've got to have a sky to look at! (p. 357)

The verse is capped by the following stage direction: "Gradually, as they speak, all light hardens to that of winter, finally" (p. 357). In realistic dialogue, Bert and Ken discuss Gus's aging and Bert's college plans. Suddenly, however, Bert disengages himself from Ken and indulges in a twelve-line soliloquy, the gist of which is that the warehouse is, in human terms, a frightening thing to contemplate. Bert wants Ken to go to school too; but the latter says: "I never could hold my mind on a far-away thing . . ." (p. 358). Ken now shows signs of spiritual decay. In another soliloquy, he expresses his contempt and bitterness for the city and its inhumanity. Finally, Ken concludes with: "And here's another grand Monday!" (p. 359). And Miller adds:

They are gradually appearing in natural light now, but it is a cold wintry light which has gradually supplanted the hot light of summer. (p. 359)

Thus, the transition is completed to the second Monday of the play. Attention has been drawn already to the small patterns and rhythms of the first Monday. Lighting—the contrast be-

tween the "hot light of summer" and the "cold wintry light"—
signals a change in tone, or emphasis, between the larger patterns, or two halves, of the play, although the underlying mood
remains constant.

On the second Monday, Bert is almost finished with *War
and Peace* and he informs Ray that he is leaving for college
on the following day. Tom, who is now a non-drinker, patron-
izingly informs Ken: "You better get yourself a little will
power. . . . You're gettin' a fine taste for the hard stuff" (p.
361). Larry speaks perhaps for the others (and possibly for
the reader) when he tells Tom: "I'm beginning to like you
better drunk" (p. 362). Patterns from the first Monday are
repeated. Once again, Eagle is coming; Gus and Jim emerge
from another weekend of drinking; and the pattern of coming
and going is renewed.

Jim explains that Gus, who removed all his money from the
bank on Friday, planned to visit his wife's grave on Saturday
but started drinking instead. Gus begs Patricia to come to
Atlantic City with him, informing her that he received five
thousand dollars insurance on his wife's death. For Patricia,
Gus is a "dirty rotten thing" (p. 365), and Tom sadly concludes that Gus lacks will power; Bert, however, says: "Gee, I
never would've thought Gus liked his wife . . ." (p. 365).

Suddenly, through the windows that have been cleaned, a
bawdy house appears across the street, and Kenneth explodes
at the reaction of his co-workers:

> Is that all yiz know . . . filthy women and dirty jokes
> and the ignorance drippin' off your faces? . . . It's an
> awful humiliation for the women here . . . a terrible
> disorganizing sight starin' a man in the face eight hours
> a day. . . . (p. 369)

Mr. Eagle says: "Shouldn't have washed the windows, I guess"
(p. 369).

Although Larry appears to be "serious" about Patricia, the girl, suspicious of the motives of a married man, does not wholly respond to him. Their relationship seems tense, fraught with doubt and cynicism (pp. 367-368). Larry later confesses that he will sell the Auburn, for it was, he says, just "one of those crazy ideas," and he admits—an irony for one who works in an auto-parts warehouse—that he "can't afford a car" (p. 371). Gus broods, too, for it troubles him that his wife died alone in the house. A vast unhappiness filling him now, Gus drinks openly on the job, not caring that Eagle sees him, and, finally he walks out of the place. This is Bert's signal for a soliloquy on the "mystery" of the warehouse, and during the soliloquy, a cone of light playing on the boy, men move "as ghostly figures, silent" in the darkness that surrounds him (pp. 370-371). When the soliloquy ends, full light returns, and the representational mode resumes. Presumably it is Tuesday now. Jim, who had accompanied Gus, returns to announce that Gus died in a cab that morning after a night of carousing.

It is time for Bert to leave, and the play draws to its close. The farewells are perfunctory: Agnes says: "good luck" (p. 374); Tom advises: "keep up the will power" (p. 374); Ray says: "'By Bert" (p. 375); and Larry manages: "Take it easy, kid" (p. 376). Kenneth, while admitting that he has been drinking heavily of late, nevertheless vows that he will go "for the Civil Service," for he will, he believes, "get back to regular there . . ."; but, unhappily, the poems he used to recite are irretrievably "gone . . . there's too much to do in this country for that kinda stuff" (p. 375). At the end, the pattern of the work accelerates in tempo:

> It is as though Bert wished it could stop for a moment, and as each person enters he looks expectantly, but nothing much happens. And so he gradually moves . . . toward an exit. . . . (p. 376)

As the curtain falls, Kenneth sings: "The minstrel boy to the war has gone!" (p. 376).

Enough has been said about the pattern of development in A *Memory of Two Mondays*. Tension results from several small problems, such as, the concealment of Tom Kelly's drunkenness from Mr. Eagle in the first Monday sequence and from larger dramatic questions, such as, will Kenneth's fate be the same as that of Gus and the other workers? One can find unifying constituents in the placement of the action on two Mondays; in Bert's reading of *War and Peace* on the first Monday and his near completion of the novel on the second Monday; in the two appearances of Mr. Eagle; in the beginning and what seems like the end of Larry's affair with Patricia; in the deterioration of Kenneth and Gus; and so forth.

The chief critical question, however, is whether Miller has succeeded in unifying his play in terms of the "two separate visions." It is important to observe that there is no preparation for the presentational transition to the second Monday. One might question not only the effectiveness of the device but also its legitimacy. In *Death of a Salesman*, Willy himself, his state of mind, provided the warrant for departures from the representational convention. Hauptmann used a dying girl's delirium in *Hannele* as a reference for projecting her fantasies. One would not wish to be dogmatic, but it would seem fitting that some kind of "logic" should prevail here. In my opinion the soliloquies add nothing to what has been apparent from the realistic dialogue and stage movement. The free verse is not only redundant, it is also undistinguished as "poetry." Bert's comparison of the warehouse to a subway (p. 358), for example, is not a very fresh or inspired image; nor would Kenneth's reference to a "lousy pork sandwich" seem to justify a departure from the basic prose convention of the play (p. 359). The "romantic" vision, and the word is Miller's (p. 333), risks tumbling into sentimentality.

Admittedly, Miller's failure to fuse the two modes of imitation in A Memory is a serious defect; but an unsatisfactory
structure does not call for a total condemnation of the piece.
Nor is the lack of "action" in a one-act work necessarily cause
for censure. Perhaps a discussion of character will suggest where
the real merit of Miller's play resides.

There are fourteen characters in A Memory of Two Mon-
days, and something has already been said about most of them.
Here I wish to focus on the four most important ones: Bert,
Kenneth, Gus, and Larry. Bert, because of his position in the
play, presents a problem. In Tennessee Williams's The Glass
Menagerie, Amanda and Laura are more memorable than Tom,
the narrator of the play. In other terms, Bert is something, as
I have said, of a novelistic "central observer"; but he is more
like, say, Jake Barnes in The Sun Also Rises than he is like
Strether in The Ambassadors; which is to say that in Miller's
play the stress is mainly on the group surrounding Bert rather
than the boy's inner world. Dialogue, consequently, fails to
record anything of note regarding Bert's background. Nevertheless, certain traits are projected.

Bert is presented as one who has an insatiable hunger for
knowledge; as has been seen, he reads Tolstoy on the subway
and he wants to take every course in the college catalog (p.
334). He is also considerate: "I always take Jim's heavy orders,
Gus" (p. 337). His courage is displayed during the first Monday sequence when Eagle is about the place, for it is Bert
who directs a flow of talk toward the unconscious Tom in an
effort to deceive the boss (p. 353). Bert is also sensitive; it
makes him "sad" to see Gus, Larry, and the others working in
the warehouse (p. 358). He feels that it would be better somehow if Kenneth went to school—thus, he has faith that the
conditions of life can be improved (p. 358). When he is leaving the warehouse, Bert reveals his loyalty and conscientious-
ness as he tells Ray: "maybe I could help you break in the
new boy" (p. 360). He shows gratitude to Larry "for teaching

[him] everything," for he admits: "I'd have been fired the first month without you, Larry" (p. 361). His perception is in evidence when he detects that beneath Gus's coarse gestures there is a genuine affection for his wife (p. 365). Humility is apparent as Bert says:

> I don't know anything:
> How is it me that gets out?
> I don't know half the poems Kenneth does,
> Or a quarter of what Larry knows about an engine.
> (p. 370)

Bert is imaginative, for he can grasp the element of "mystery" in life. He lacks, however, the knowledge, the vocabulary, and the maturity that would enable him to enunciate a more adequate explanation than he gives for that "mystery":

> Gee, it's peculiar to leave a place—forever!
> Still, I always hated coming here;
> . . . .
> I know I'll remember them as long as I live,
> As long as I live they'll never die,
> And still I know that in a month or two
> They'll forget my name, and mix me up
> With another boy who worked here once,
> And went. Gee, it's a mystery! (p. 371)

"Gee" (as Willy Loman put it) "is a boy's word." Moreover, Miller himself has asked for a drama that transcends the limited perspective of the adolescent, and he has also commented on "mystery." In "The Shadows of the Gods" in *Harper's*, August 1958, for example, he says: "The mystery of our condition remains, but we know much more about it than appears on our stage."

Bert, then, is depicted as a likeable young man. All the same, he remains a flat character because he is almost too good to be true. The other characters have faults; Bert has none. (Huck Finn is an engaging boy, too—he is also an inveterate liar.) Nor does Bert grow; his position at the end of a year is about the same as when the play started.

Kenneth is described in the following terms:

> [He] is twenty-six, a strapping, fair-skinned man, with thinning hair, delicately shy, very strong. He has only recently come to this country. (p. 338)

Kenneth brings with him into the warehouse the fresh breath of an older and contrasting culture; incongruously juxtaposed with the cramped, dusty warehouse is Ken's remembrance of open country, poetry, and God. He quotes Norman McLeod, but he refers to poetry as a "useless" Irish occupation (p. 339). He says:

> Why, it's the poetry hour, Gus . . . the hour all men rise to thank God for the blue of the sky, the roundness of the everlasting globe, and the cheerful cleanliness of the subway system. . . . Oh, Bert, I never thought I would end me life wrappin' brown paper around strange axles. (p. 339)

Kenneth has a sense of humor; but it is one sign of his deterioration that his humor begins to fade perceptively in the play's second half (p. 361). He is also poor; he wears used shoes that cost a quarter; when Gus rebukes him for complaining, Kenneth says: "Oh, when I'm rich, Gus, I'll have very little more to say" (p. 343). Kenneth is not solely concerned with material deprivations; he is equally concerned with the spiritual poverty of his situation: "There's a good deal of monotony connected with the life," he says, ". . . And no philosophical idea at all, y'know, to pass the time" (p. 347). Kenneth is a bit of a "dreamer"; he is not portrayed as the wholly victimized. When Bert asks: "Didn't you ever want to be anything, Kenneth?" the reply is: "I've never been able to keep my mind on it, Bert" (p. 358). On the second Monday, Kenneth has forgotten "the bloody poems. . . . It's the drinkin' does it . . . I've got to stop the drinkin'!" (p. 359). There is a suggestion that Kenneth resents Bert's leaving (p. 360); his own hope is Civil Service—but:

> I've a feelin' I'd never dare leave it, y'know? And I'm not ready for me last job yet. . . . I don't want nothin' to be the last, yet. (p. 360)

The brothel across the street is the final offense against Kenneth's "romantic" conception of life: "I'd sooner roll myself around in the horse manure of the gutter!" (p. 367). At the end, he has decided on Civil Service; he has also adjusted himself to the mice in the place: "they've got to live, too, I suppose" (p. 376). In other words, Kenneth has adjusted himself to "reality"; nevertheless, as the curtain falls, the Irishman continues to sing.

Gus is individualized in vivid terms:

> a barrel-bellied man, totally bald, with a long, fierce, gray mustache that droops on the right side. He wears a bowler, and his pants are a little too short. He has a ready-made clip-on tie. He wears winter underwear all summer long, changes once a week. There is something neat and dusty about him—a rolling gait, bandy legs, a belly hard as a rock and full of beer. He speaks with a gruff Slavic accent. (p. 336)

Gus has been a rate clerk with the company for twenty-two years, and he relates his history in the following manner:

> Them mice was here before [Bert] was born. . . . When

Mr. Eagle was in high school I was already here. When there was Winton Six I was here. When was Minerva car I was here. When was Stanley Steamer I was here, and Stearns Knight, and Marmon was good car; I was here all them times. I was here first day Raymond come; he was young boy; work hard be manager. When Agnes still think she was gonna get married I was here. When was Locomobile, and Model K Ford and Model N Ford —all them different Fords, and Franklin was good car, Jordon car, Reo car, Pierce Arrow, Cleveland car—all them was good cars. All them times I was here. (p. 370)

Gus's drinking and whoring may be viewed as symptomatic of his boredom and frustration. That Gus has not been entirely brutalized, however, is evident from the fact that he takes a protective stance toward Jim and Tom, and that his wife's death is an event that signals the beginning of the end for him. On the second Monday, then, Gus seems suddenly older; he has grown quiet and moody (p. 358). The hostile side of his ambivalent attitude toward the firm increasingly manifests itself; he too begins to complain of the mice and the dirt (p. 364); and he drinks openly—even defiantly—on the job (p. 368). After withdrawing all his money from the bank, he says: "What for I put in bank? I'm sixty-eight years old . . . I got no children, nothing . . ." (p. 364). After twenty-two years, then, Gus finishes with—"nothing." Like Willy Loman, Gus feels that his life has been a failure; his farewell orgy is an attempt, grotesque as it might be, to end his life in a meaningful fashion: "I'm gonna do it right," he asserts (p. 373). And "doing it right" means more than the mere sense of potency he derives from squandering his life's savings, or from whoring and drinking; it means—and this is the important thing—phone calls to distant relatives and war-time buddies; for it is an inarticulate stretching after the warmth of human love, or "comradeship." At the end, then, Gus tries to snatch some significance from the life that is growing dark around him. Ironically, however, instead of the warmth of human love Gus catches a chill and dies in the rear seat of a taxi cab. "It was," says Jim, "just gettin' to be morning" (p. 372).

Larry "is thirty-nine, a troubled but phlegmatic man, good-looking" (p. 341). Larry gains a sense of self-importance by purchasing an Auburn and by sleeping with Patricia. Here, too, then, motivation is symptomatic; for Larry is tired of being "careful" (p. 345). A stronger and more intelligent man might have found constructive outlets for his discontent; but Larry is not very bright:

> Gus: You crazy? Buy Auburn?
> Larry, *with depth—a profound conclusion*: I like the valves, Gus. (p. 342)

Whether or not Larry can sell the car later is not important— nor is it important, finally, that he is pressed for money: "The car put me a hundred and thirty bucks in the hole. If one of the kids gets sick I'll be strapped" (p. 345). There is, it seems, no lasting escape from facts; when Larry decides to sell the Auburn, he admits defeat (p. 367). Similarly, although Larry claims to be "serious" about Patricia, the affair appears unsatisfactory because the lovers are merely exploiting each other; this is suggested when Larry warns Patricia that she might end her days in the whorehouse across the street—and the whorehouse is the symbol for the ultimate in human exploitation (p. 368).

Bert, Kenneth, Gus, and Larry are richly orchestrated. As the quotations above should illustrate, speech in the play is highly diversified; the prose dialogue is clearly superior to the pretentious free verse excursions. The language of Kenneth and Gus is particularly effective, and both men's speech patterns are contrasted with the New York City accents of the other characters (Tom Kelly being the one exception). As different as Kenneth and Gus appear at first sight, one can yet discern the suggestion that Kenneth might very well go the way of the Slav. Dialogue would appear to relate as much as necessary about Kenneth and Gus—about their backgrounds and attitudes—to make their actions consistent and credible. Although Bert (and the secondary characters) remain fixed, Kenneth and Gus disintegrate before our eyes, while Larry renounces the Auburn and apparently arrives at a new stage in his relations with Patricia. Although the minor figures are flat, they are individualized and all together they present a convincing picture of the chosen scene. Perhaps in no other Miller play, with the exception of *Salesman,* has the playwright depicted such robust figures. Perhaps the abandonment of "plot" permitted Miller to relax and lavish more care on character; nor are reasons personal to the author to be overlooked ("I love nothing printed here," says Miller, "better than this play" [p. 49 in the "Introduction"]). But how representative are these characters? And how well do they reveal the theme of the play? In his introduction to the original edition of *A Memory,* Miller says that "in this play the warehouse is our world—a world in which things are endlessly sent and endlessly received; only time never comes back." In the play itself, however, as has been said, Bert compares the warehouse to a subway, and the subway, in turn, becomes a paradigm for "all of us in the world." How adequate are these symbols?

The subway, I have suggested, is not a fortunate image. The chief reason for this is that it is not made concrete in the play —it is simply verbalized in an abstract way. It is also, together with its cognate image the railroad, a tired literary symbol. The warehouse scene, on the other hand, is another matter, for it is rendered in concrete terms—it is, in short, very much "there" and, consequently, the theme, aided by some memorable characterization, is made vivid and palpable. The warehouse, then, provides not only unity of place but unity of theme.

Miller, speaking ironically of course, says:

> The play speaks not of obsession but of rent and hunger and the need for a little poetry in life and is entirely out of date in those respects. . . . ("Introduction," p. 49)

The play, as I see it, is not seriously dated in any respect. For one thing, A Memory does speak of "obsession"—many of Miller's characters are obsessed with drink and sex. At the present moment, government statistics indicate that the poverty group in the United States embraces some thirty-five million people. Nor would Miller's symbol appear to be limited to what the playwright refers to as "that sub-culture where the sinews of the economy are rooted" (p. 49). Evidently, Miller made his play unfold on two Mondays because he wanted to underscore the relationship between work (the week) and play (the weekend). Miller's workers have an ambivalent attitude toward the company. On the weekend, they seek escape from meaninglessness and monotony through drink and sex; but, finding no significance in their "free time," either, they crawl back to work, hoping perhaps to find there some relief from their agonizing sense of emptiness. One reason that the lyric interludes verge on sentimentality is the fact that they fail to probe more deeply than the action itself into the reasons for man's fate in this particular environment. The interludes merely substitute adolescent gush about "mystery" for more penetrating analysis and reflection. (There is "mystery" in life, but, as I have suggested, Bert would not seem adequate to the task of telling us about it.) Although the warehouse offers the workers a bond of pseudo-community lacking elsewhere, it fails finally to provide them with any real feeling of belonging. The result is the perpetuation of the weary round of futility and loneliness.

Is the picture presented here "dated"? Is it unique to a "sub-culture"? C. Wright Mills, in his study of the modern American middle class, says:

> Each day men sell little pieces of themselves in order to try to buy them back each night and week-end with the coin of "fun." The week-end, having nothing in common with the working week, lifts men and women out of the gray level tone of everyday work life, and forms a standard with which the working life is contrasted.

But Mills adds:

> The amusement of hollow people rests on their own hollowness and does not fill them up; it does not calm or relax them, as old middle class frolics and jollification may have done; it does not re-create their spontaneity in work, as in the craftsman model. . . .

It is the "craftsman model," perhaps, that Miller sees supplanted by the "ghostly figures" of his play. No doubt a good deal of nonsense has been written about the "craftsman model"; it is nevertheless true that the "industrial model" has contributed to that revulsion of modern life which is perhaps the distinctive literary vision of our time. With the introduction of the whorehouse, Miller achieves, on the thematic level, unity of focus, for the two worlds of work and play are fused in a symbolic manner as the noose of alienation and exploitation is drawn tighter and the strangling forces of dehumanization are almost completed.

The essentially impersonal quality of group relations in an industrial society is conveyed in a telling way by the death of Gus:

Kenneth: Gus died.
Frank: No kiddin'!
Kenneth: Ya, last night.
Frank: What do you know. Hm. *He goes on picking packages out.* Is this all for West Bronx, Tom?
Tom: I guess so for now.
Frank, *to Kenneth:* Died.
Kenneth: Yes, Jim was with him. Last night.
Frank: Jesus. *Pause. He stares, shakes his head.* I'll take Brooklyn when I get back, Tommy. *He goes out, loaded with packages.* (pp. 373-374)

Although Gus gave twenty-two years of his life to the company, his death must not be permitted to impede the march of the industrial machine—the West Bronx and Brooklyn must be serviced. There is neither time, nor apparently inclination, or inner resources, to lament for Gus, to cry out in anger, to unravel the meaning and the moral from the inhuman pattern of his life and death. There is more here, evidently, than the universal mute sense of dread that all men feel in the presence of death, for there is a social dimension to the problem. One cog in a vast machine has ceased functioning; but no matter—the cog will be replaced, even as Bert will be replaced. It is the gross output of material production and distribution that is important, not specifically human concerns. Kenneth's remark—"And no philosophical idea at all, y'know, to pass the time" (p. 347)—is, because it sums up the spiritual poverty of Miller's workers, pertinent here. True, Miller's extra-dramatic remarks on the warehouse ("a world in which things are endlessly sent and endlessly received".) may seem a bit strained as a symbol of our time, and though "only time never comes back" may be true of any age, in the play itself, I repeat, the warehouse seems to be a faithful reflector of the modern condition.

Nor can *A Memory* be dismissed as a mere "remnant of

social protest," with the inference that it is a rehash of work dating from the Thirties. Compare Miller's play with Odets's *Waiting for Lefty* or even *Awake and Sing!*; there is no call to arms in Miller's play; no glib oversimplified solutions; and no stock capitalistic bosses—Ray is human and even Eagle, though seemingly indifferent to the whorehouse, gives Tom Kelly another opportunity to redeem himself and seems to be extremely patient with what Ray calls a "circus around here" (p. 365). The play, while it stresses social necessity, by no means excludes conscious will, for as Miller himself points out in the "Introduction": "from this endless, timeless, will-less environment, a boy emerges who will not accept its defeat or its mood as final . . ." (p. 49). One might also point to Kenneth, who is not only a victim of a new society but is prey to his own weak will as well. As in *Salesman*, Miller is attempting, within the limits imposed by his brief form, to give the "whole truth."

In his "Introduction," Miller defines his play as a "pathetic comedy" (p. 49). Although it cannot be affirmed that Miller has "hit a target" in every respect here, for the structure is defective in its failure to knit the "two separate visions" of the play, or that the play is a major work of dramatic art, still, a reasonably successful "pathetic comedy," it seems to me, is a modest claim to make for *A Memory of Two Mondays*.

CHAPTER FIVE

A View from the Bridge

When A View from the Bridge (1955) had its première in New York it was, like A Memory of Two Mondays (which was on the same bill), a one-act play. Miller was dissatisfied with this version, however, and by the time that the play had its London opening (1956) it had grown to the dimensions of two acts. In this study the text will be the final version as it appears in the Collected Plays, but a Note at the end of the chapter will briefly compare the two versions in some important respects.

In his "Introduction" to the first version of A View from the Bridge, Miller expressed his wish to capture a plot curve, a "breathtaking simplicity" through a "clear, clean line of . . . catastrophe":

> the form announces in the first moments of the play that only that will be told which is cogent, and that this story is the only part of Eddie Carbone's life worth our notice and therefore no effort will be made to draw in elements of his life that are beneath these, the most tense and meaningful of his hours. (pp. 17-18)

Although Miller says that he "modified" the "original frieze-like character" in the second version of A View, that he came to identify himself more closely with the experience he was depicting and gave more prominence to characters other than the hero, he says nothing about abandoning his original desire for a "clear, clean line of" development (pp. 17-18). I will attempt to show that A *View's* plot curve is deceptively simple.

The title of Miller's play suggests the importance of point of view in the structure of the work. In this play, Miller supplies the warrant for his departures from a representational mode of imitation by placing on stage a chorus-character, Alfieri, who introduces the action, functions as one of the characters in that action, comments on the action from a point outside the enactment, and serves as a transitional agent between scenes and acts. Point of view alternates, then, between a subjective, or presentational reference (Alfieri's first-person direct statements to the audience and his interpretation of events) and objective, or representational reference (the "third-person" direct "statement" of that action which is its own commentary, including scenes in which Alfieri functions as an actor and not as a chorus).

The setting, which is an important factor in a play that alternates between different modes of imitation, is described as follows:

> The street and house front of a tenement building. The front is skeletal entirely. The main acting area is the living room-dining room of Eddie's apartment. It is a worker's flat, clean, sparse, homely. . . .
> At back are a bedroom door and an opening to the kitchen; none of these interiors are seen.
> At the right, forestage, a desk. This is Mr. Alfieri's law office.
> There is also a telephone booth. This is not used until the last scenes, so it may be covered or left in view.
> A stairway leads up to the apartment, and then farther up to the next story, which is not seen.
> Ramps, representing the street, run upstage and off to right and left. (p. 378)

In Act Two, some part of the stage is used as "the reception room of a prison" (p. 433).

Time in A *View* is presented in a straightforward manner. Act One covers a period of several weeks; Alfieri relates this once as commentator (p. 397) and Bea confirms it in dialogue (p. 399). Eleven days pass during Act Two; the curtain rises on December 23rd (Alfieri as commentator is the authority here, p. 418); Marco and Rodolpho are arrested on December 27th (for Alfieri's reference to the date, see p. 423), and on that date it is announced in dialogue that Catherine will marry Rodolpho in one week (p. 427); on the girl's wedding day—a week later, then—the play ends (p. 439). The meaning of these events and the identification of these characters will become clear in a moment.

Perhaps the best approach to A *View* would involve an explication of the text in terms of point of attack, exposition, foreshadowing, complication, transition, turning point, crisis, climax, and conclusion. After the analysis of the structure proper, there will be a brief discussion of the specific pictorial devices that Miller has employed in a effort to highlight Eddie Carbone as protagonist. Some comment on the use of irony in the play will follow. The problem of Alfieri's role in the play can be more profitably debated later in the chapter. Close analysis of structure should furnish a basis for evaluating Miller's achievement here; it should also establish a reference point for criticisms of the play that will be considered in the discussion of theme.

ACT ONE

The curtain rises on two longshoremen, Louis and Mike, who are pitching coins in front of Eddie's house. The sound of a foghorn reminds us that the bay is near; it also helps to establish the mood of the play. Alfieri appears, comes down

to his desk, and introduces himself to the audience. Red Hook,
Brooklyn, he says, used to be an uncivilized neighborhood—
"there were many here who were justly shot by unjust men" (p.
379); but now the section is "quite civilized, quite American.
Now we settle for half and we like it better" (p. 379). (This
is more than exposition; it is also preparation for the contrast
between the Old World code of Sicily and early Red Hook—
represented chiefly by Marco—and the New World code enun-
ciated by Alfieri; the importance of these two codes will become
apparent in the course of the play.) Alfieri then introduces
Eddie Carbone as one whose fate was unique in later day
"civilized" Red Hook. (Preparation.) Eddie appears; and, as
Eddie enters the house, Alfieri disappears into darkness.

Light rises on the apartment. Catherine, Eddie's niece, appears before her uncle in her new clothes; the latter is critical,
however, about her short skirt, about her walk, and about her
attentions to a young fellow. Catherine objects that Eddie is
always negative toward her male friends. (Exposition; also
preparation for Eddie's insane jealousy over Rodolpho.) Eddie
sends for his wife, Bea; he wants to tell her that her cousins
have arrived illegally from Italy; the cousins are going to stay
with the Carbones. Eddie is informed that Catherine has been
offered a job; but once again, Eddie is disapproving—the neighborhood is bad, the company is inferior in status, and the like.
This time, however, Catherine fights back and Eddie is forced
to consent. (Complication; Catherine's insistence on her rights
will eventually force Eddie to take an extreme position in his
efforts to control his niece.) Eddie warns the women never to
mention the cousins to anyone on the outside; he tells Catherine about a boy who "snitched to the Immigration" on his
uncle; in revenge, his own family "pulled him down the
stairs. . . . And they spit on him in the street . . ." (pp. 388-
389). (Preparation for Eddie's betrayal of the cousins; by stressing the seriousness of the code and by showing the consequences of breaking that code, Miller heightens suspense and

the sense of expectation. The major dramatic question is also insinuated: Would Eddie, who has an unacknowledged lust for Catherine, ever be jealously provoked into betraying his wife's family? And if he betrayed them, what results would follow? Would he achieve insight into his motivation? Would it lead to his death? This is the point of attack. There are roughly thirty-eight pages of dialogue in Act One, and the attack occurs in the eleventh page.) Eddie, alone in his rocker then, looks at his watch; like a cinematic dissolve, the lights go down on Eddie . . . and rise on Alfieri.

Alfieri picks up the dissolve suggestion of time and bridges the hours until ten o'clock that night. Light fades on Alfieri . . . and rises on Marco and Rodolpho in front of Eddie's house.

Rodolpho, Marco's younger brother, is impressed by the appearance of the Carbone house. (Preparation for Rolopho's decision to stay in America, which leads to conflict with Eddie over Catherine.) Marco knocks. Light rises on the apartment; Eddie goes to the door. Light fades on the street. . . .

Marco and Rodolpho explain how difficult life is in Italy. (Exposition; clearer motivation for Rodolpho's decision to stay in America, but also motivation for the violence of Marco's reaction to Eddie's betrayal.) Rodolpho is not married. (Preparation for the love affair between Catherine and Rodolpho.) Catherine encourages Rodolpho to sing "Paper Doll." (This is an example of irony that will be discussed below.) Nervously, Eddie quiets the singer, who has captivated Catherine, by professing the fear that noise might arouse unwanted curiosity. (Eddie's jealousy and the theme of betrayal touch here between the lines.) The scene ends with Eddie watching the couple laughing together . . . and the "room dies" (p. 397).

Light rises on Alfieri. The lawyer suggests the dangerous course that Eddie will pursue; he also bridges the several weeks that have passed. Light, then, fades on Alfieri . . .

Light rises on Eddie—then Bea—in front of the house. Eddie is worried about Catherine, who is out with Rodolpho. (Complication.) Eddie denies to Bea that he is jealous of Rodolpho; he says that he simply does not like the boy; Rodolpho, Eddie claims, is effeminate. (Preparation for the line of attack Eddie will take against Rodolpho.) Bea complains that Eddie has been cold sexually toward her for months; Eddie is evasive on the subject. (This reveals the underside of Eddie's "madonna complex"; because there is a definite sexual motive—though repressed—in Eddie's love for his niece, we are ready for the kiss he gives the girl in Act Two; furthermore, the dark strength of that love makes Eddie's betrayal of the cousins, with all that that betrayal implies, more credible.) Louis and Mike appear, and in a guarded fashion they mock the antics of Rodolpho. (The relevance of this scene will be discussed in the final section of the chapter.) Suddenly Rodolpho and Catherine appear. Once again, Eddie is disapproving; but, after the boy has gone, Eddie goes farther—he tells Catherine that Rodolpho is only using her as a means to stay in America. (Preparation for the second line of attack Eddie takes against Rodolpho.) But Catherine defends Rodolpho in strong terms. (Conflict; and preparation for a continuing struggle of wills between Catherine and Eddie.) The two then go upstairs and . . . light rises on the apartment.

Alone with Catherine, Bea warns the girl that she must escape Eddie's influence; she adds that Catherine is partly to blame because she forgets that she is a woman now. (This complicates the conflict because Catherine is seen to contribute to the problem; moreover, Catherine's inner conflict, her wish to escape Eddie's influence and her wish to be dependent, assure that a change, one way or the other, must come about.)

"Lights out on them and up on Alfieri, seated behind his desk" (p. 406). Eddie visits Alfieri; he wants to know if something legal can be done about Rodolpho who, he suspects, is using Catherine. (Complication; Eddie is taking a more determined, more overt line now against his antagonist.) Alfieri says that there is no legal problem here. Eddie insists that Rodolpho "ain't right"; he says: "you could kiss him he [is] so sweet" (p. 408). (Preparation for Eddie's kissing Rodolpho in Act Two.) Alfieri insists: "You have no recourse in the law, Eddie" (p. 408). (Preparation for Eddie's action against Rodolpho outside the law.) Alfieri hints that Eddie would not wish to report Rodolpho; and Eddie is horrified at the suggestion. (Preparation.) When Alfieri urges Eddie to release Catherine, Eddie exits resentfully. Alfieri, facing the audience, points out the inevitability of the tragedy. Light fades on Alfieri . . .

Light rises on the living room "where all are finishing dinner" (p. 410). Once again, the cousins discuss the poverty in Italy. (Strong motivation for Marco's revenge against Eddie.) Eddie asks Marco whether Italian women remain faithful to their men when the latter are away from home. Most of them do, answers Marco; and Rodolpho adds: "It's more strict in our town" (p. 412). Eddie replies: "It ain't so free here either, Rodolpho, like you think" (p. 412). (Open conflict.) Catherine plays "Paper Doll" and encourages Rodolpho to dance with her; while they dance, Marco informs Eddie that in Italy, when the men go out on fishing trips, Rodolpho does the cooking. Eddie jokes: "He sings, he cooks, he could make dresses . . ." (p. 414); but beneath his words, Eddie is ready to explode. Abruptly, Eddie rises and suggests taking Marco and Rodolpho to the fights on Saturday night. He offers to teach Rodolpho how to box; the two men spar a bit; then Eddie "feints with his left and lands with his right. It mildly staggers Rodolpho" (p. 416). Eddie says: "I'll teach him again." (Preparation for more conflict.) Marco faces Eddie, then, and challenges him to lift a chair by grasping only the bottom of one leg. Eddie fails to raise the chair; but Marco lifts the chair over his head:

> Marco is face to face with Eddie . . . the chair raised like a weapon over Eddie's head—and he transforms what might appear like a glare of warning into a smile

of triumph, and Eddie's grin vanishes as he absorbs his look. (p. 417)

CURTAIN

(This scene looks forward to the resolution of the play.)

ACT TWO

Light rises on Alfieri, who sets the stage for the next scene; it is two days before Christmas; Catherine and Rodolpho are alone in the apartment . . .

"Light is rising on Catherine . . . Rodolpho is watching as she arranges a paper pattern on cloth spread on the table" (p. 418). Rodolpho asks Catherine to marry him; the girl, however, is afraid of Eddie. (The threat of violence creates suspense.) She does not, moreover, want to hurt Eddie. (Complication.) She asks Rodolpho if he would marry her if they had to live in Italy; his reply is in the negative because such a marriage would not be sensible. Rodolpho urges Catherine to break free of Eddie's influence; but the girl remains confused. Rodolpho leads her into the bedroom . . .

Light rises on the street. Eddie appears, drunk. (Preparation.) Eddie enters the apartment: "He sees the pattern and cloth, goes over to it and touches it, and turns toward upstage" (p. 421). Catherine issues from the bedroom, smoothing her dress. (Preparation.) Rodolpho follows—and Eddie immediately grasps the situation. He orders Rodolpho to pack and leave. When Catherine asserts that she will leave too, Eddie blocks her path:

Catherine: Eddie, I'm not gonna be a baby any more!
You—

He reaches out suddenly, draws her to him, and as she
strives to free herself he kisses her on the mouth.
(p. 422)

(Conflict and complication; for the first time, Eddie clearly
reveals the naked lust behind his love for the girl.) As Rodolpho tries to stop Eddie, the latter taunts him about his
effeminancy:

Rodolpho flies at him in attack. Eddie pins his arms,
laughing, and suddenly kisses him. (p. 422)

(Strong conflict that realizes previous preparation.) Eddie and
Rodolpho glare at each other "like animals that have torn at
one another and broken up without a decision . . ." (p. 423).
(Promise of continuing conflict.) Eddie warns Rodolpho:

Watch your step. . . . By rights they oughta throw you
back in the water. But I got pity for you. (p. 423)

(Preparation for the crisis of the play when Eddie betrays the
cousins.) Light fades on the apartment . . .
    Alfieri bridges the four days that have passed. Eddie enters;
he claims to have proof that Rodolpho "ain't right" because
the boy did not try, says Eddie, to break his grip. Alfieri says:
"It sounds like he just wasn't strong enough to break your
grip" (p. 424). (Complication; Eddie is growing more desperate.) The lawyer urges Eddie, more strongly this time, to
release Catherine:

The law is nature. The law is only a word for what has
a right to happen. . . . Let her go. . . . A phone booth
begins to glow on the opposite side of the stage; a faint
lonely blue. . . . Eddie starts turning to go and Alfieri
rises with new anxiety. You won't have a friend in the

> world, Eddie! . . . *Eddie moves off* . . . *[Alfieri] follows*
> *into the darkness, calling desperately. Eddie is gone. The*
> *phone is glowing in light now. Light is out on Alfieri.*
> *Eddie has at the same time appeared beside the phone.*
> (p. 424)

(This is the turning point of the play. It looks back to the
point of attack and forward to the resolution.) Eddie calls
the Immigration Bureau. As Eddie leaves the phone booth,
Louis and Mike appear. (The juxtaposition here suggests
Alfieri's warning—which was, in turn, prepared for at the
point of attack in the story about the boy who betrayed his
uncle, and once again, looks forward to the end of the play.)
Eddie goes upstairs.

Light rises on the apartment. Bea informs Eddie that Catherine will marry Rodolpho in a week. He is also told that the
cousins have moved upstairs with two other aliens. He is
shocked at this; for he fears that if the Immigration officers
trap the second pair of aliens the family will seek revenge
against him. (Suspense.) The officers enter, then, and search
the building. Bea is certain that Eddie has betrayed the men.
The officers return with the four aliens. Marco spits in Eddie's
face. (Realizes previous preparation.) Eddie threatens to kill
Marco. (Promise of continuing conflict and preparation for
the climax.) Marco points to Eddie: "He killed my children!
That one stole the food from my children!" (p. 433). (This
again underscores the motivation for Marco.) The crowd de-
serts Eddie. (Realizes previous preparation.)

Lights up on a prison. Alfieri tries to secure Marco's promise
not to start a fight with Eddie if he is permitted to attend his
brother's wedding. Marco says: "In my country he would be
dead now" (p. 433). (This continues the contrast between
codes announced at the start of the play, the theme of which
runs throughout the two acts.) Alfieri says that nothing can

be done about Eddie. Marco says: "All the law is not in a book"; but Alfieri replies: "There is no other law" (p. 434). (Complication.) Finally, Marco promises not to start trouble. (The threat, however, remains.)

Light rises on the apartment. Eddie refuses to attend the wedding unless Marco apologizes. Enter Rodolpho; he begs Eddie's pardon for not asking permission to court Catherine; he wants to kiss Eddie's hand, but the latter says: "I want my name . . . Marco's got my name. . . . Take me to him" (p. 437). (Preparation for the climax.) Bea says: "That's not what you want. . . . You want somethin' else . . . and you can never have her!" (p. 437). (This is the crisis of the play. It focuses for the last time, and in ultimate terms, the question of Eddie's unacknowledged motivation. Will he admit the truth now? What will be the result of his conflict with Marco?) Eddie and Catherine are both shocked. Marco appears, outside . . .

Action moves into the area in front of Eddie's house. Eddie and Marco fight—and Eddie is fatally stabbed with his own knife. (This is the climax of the play.) Eddie, without ever acknowledging the real nature of his love for Catherine, dies. Alfieri steps forward from the crowd around the fallen Eddie, and, enclosed in a cone of light, the lawyer delivers Eddie's requiem. (This thematically important speech, together with its explication will appear in the final pages of this chapter.) (The conclusion of the play.)

CURTAIN

Eddie Carbone's dominant position in the play is emphasized by a number of "external" devices. When first introduced, Eddie "is highlighted among" the men against Alfieri's oral presentation (p. 379). When the first scene in the apartment ends, Eddie is *alone* for a moment before the scene changes; this visual image does more than merely focus the chief actor, it is a foreshadowing of his coming isolation (p. 390). When the first scene with the cousins ends, "Eddie is downstage [read "highlighted"] . . . and the room dies" (p. 397). At the first act curtain, the focus is on Eddie's vanishing grin—which means that the actor impersonating Eddie would have to be placed in a manner that would permit Eddie to be "highlighted" (p. 417). In Act Two, when Rodolpho leads Catherine to the bedroom, Eddie appears below, *alone* (p. 421). The following scene concludes on Eddie's line and his exit (p. 423). When Eddie leaves Alfieri's office, the latter keeps calling Eddie's name (p. 424). When Eddie next appears, he is *alone* in the phone booth (p. 424). The auditory and visual effects in these last two instances powerfully "highlight" Eddie. When Marco and Rodolpho are apprehended, the scene goes dark with Eddie calling after them (p. 433). After the scene in the prison, light rises on Eddie *alone* in his apartment (p. 435). The effect of isolation from the group is very strong in this instance. The play ends—as it began—with Alfieri's comments focused on the fate of Eddie Carbone.

Dialogue is not limited to exposition and foreshadowing in the narrow functional sense here, for irony is extremely dense in this play. In respect to Eddie's allowing the cousins to stay with him, Bea says: "you'll get a blessing for this!" (p. 383); Act Two starts two days before Christmas—and Eddie's "blessing" becomes evident when he discovers Catherine and Rodolpho alone in the apartment. When Rodolpho appears on the scene, Eddie says: "[Catherine's] a baby, how is she gonna know what she likes?"; to which Bea replies: "Well you kept her a baby, you wouldn't let her go out" (p. 427). At a dark moment Bea says: "a wedding should be happy!" (p. 428). It was Bea, too, who said, earlier: "It's very good news, Eddie. I want you to be happy . . . Catherine's got a job" (p. 384). The "Paper Doll" song functions in two ways: first it makes

Rodolpho appear silly (more on Rodolpho's "ambiguity" below); second—and this is perhaps more important—the song is a comment on Eddie; for he has made a "doll" out of Catherine, he is "alone," and he wants a "doll that other fellows cannot steal" (p. 396). Note that "Paper Doll" is played again at the end of Act One (pp. 416-417), which foreshadows the climax of the play. This ironic motif is carefully introduced in Act Two through the "paper pattern on cloth" that Catherine is fashioning (p. 418). Eddie's reaction to the pattern was quoted above; and when Eddie "turns toward upstage," he turns, in effect, toward the loss of his "paper doll." Observe also that Miller gives the theme a complicating turn of the screw; Eddie asks Catherine: "Rodolpho makin' you a dress?" (p. 421); Eddie, as I shall argue later, is shifting the guilt he feels for his neuroticism concerning his niece onto Rodolpho's alleged abnormality. There is a good deal of verbal play in A View. At one point, Eddie asks Bea whether she is "mad" at him; Bea replies: "You're the one is mad" (p. 390). After arguing with Eddie over the job offer, Catherine lights her uncle's cigar; says Eddie: "Don't burn yourself" (p. 390). Eddie claims that Rodolpho lacks "respect" for Catherine; but after Eddie kisses his niece in the second act, Rodolpho says: "Have respect for her!" (p. 422). The first meeting between Catherine and Rodolpho ends thus:

> Catherine: You like sugar?
> Rodolpho: Sugar? Yes! I like sugar very much!
>   Eddie is downstage, watching as she pours a spoonful of sugar into his cup, his face puffed with trouble, and the room dies. (p. 397)

At one point, Eddie says: "she is my niece and I'm responsible for her"; and Bea says: "What you done to him in front of her . . . that's what you call responsible for her?" (p. 426).

Eddie insists: "I only wanted the *best* for you, Katie" (p. 428, italics mine). In the prison scene, there is an important ironic stroke:

> Alfieri: To promise not to kill is not dishonorable.
> Marco, *looking at Alfieri*: No?
> Alfieri: No.
> Marco, *gesturing with his head*—this is a new idea. . . .
> (P. 434)

Alfieri obviously intends something different from Marco's interpretation of the statement. Finally, the play draws to its close on an ironic note:

> Catherine: Eddie I never meant to do nothing bad to you.
> Eddie: Then why—Oh, B.!
> Beatrice: Yes, yes!
> Eddie: My B.!
> (P. 439)

Eddie dies blank as ever on his motivations; he continues to feel that Catherine did something "bad" to him; his last gasp—"My B.!"—reveals his deep confusion about the object of his desires.

In A *View from the Bridge,* point of view alternates between subjective and objective reference in a consistent manner (something that cannot always be affirmed of *Death of a Salesman,* though it must be owned that the earlier play is a more complex performance). Exposition and foreshadowing through dialogue are expert; there are no awkward surprises; the development is credible and the transitions are smooth. Lighting, though highly effective in its cinematic fluidity, fails to characterize or establish mood to any significant degree; nor are sound effects often called for in the text (in this respect the play is

also inferior to *Salesman*). The London criticism that Act One
is slow in building tension receives scant support from the
text. Aside from Alfieri's direct statements, which are calculated
to arouse interest, there is the enactment itself, which projects
conflict from the first page of dialogue (Eddie's argument with
Catherine); the discussion about the cousins begins on the
second page of dialogue, with the danger of the operation suggested on the third page; conflict occurs again on page five in
the dispute about Catherine's job—and so it goes, in ascending
waves, throughout the play. The point of attack, as I have
indicated, occurs fairly early in the play. It has been said that
A *View* is repetitious. My analysis of Eddie's development and
the ensuing plot complications, however, refute the charge.
Arthur Ganz criticizes the final scene because, as he sees it,
Eddie's love for Catherine abruptly vanishes and is replaced by
his love for Bea. Apparently the irony of the ending eludes
Mr. Ganz. It also eludes Robert Hogan, who says that the
"reconciliation" between man and wife, while it renders Eddie
more "normal," also reduces his stature. That the ending of
A *View from the Bridge* is part of an ironic structure-texture
complex is clear from the samples given above. Finally, Miller's
control is manifest in his formal patterning of scenes and acts
—the relationship between the ending of Act One and the
climax of the play is not an isolated instance—and in his
mastery of focus on Eddie Carbone as protagonist.

And it is time now to take a closer look at this protagonist.
Eddie Carbone, according to Miller's stage directions, is "forty
—a husky, slightly overweight longshoreman" (p. 379). Evidently Eddie is a hard worker (p. 390) and a good boxer
(p. 415). Unhappily, however, Eddie is the victim of a rather
well-known neurotic conflict. His sexual desire for his niece
functions as an incestuous fixation, inasmuch as Catherine's
role is like a daughter's within the family constellation; this
repressed desire—nakedly exposed in the kissing scene of Act
Two—prompts Eddie's defense mechanism, the "Madonna

complex." It is a defense mechanism (so an analyst of the
Freudian school would argue) because it is contrived to protect
Catherine, and Eddie himself, from the forbidden desires. Various elements in the play underline this "high-low" dichotomy
in Eddie (or the split between the "sacred" and the "profane").
For example, possessiveness *and* the split can be seen when
Eddie disparages the "low" neighborhood in which Catherine
must work; when he criticizes the "low" kind of business
(plumbing—which is associated with excretory and, through
propinquity, sexual functions); when he objects to her visiting
Times Square because it is "full of tramps" (p. 401). Miller
suggests that Eddie is in the grip of a "repetition compulsion,"
that is, that Eddie is reliving through Catherine an original
Oedipal situation; Eddie is described, in one place, as looking at
Catherine "like a lost boy" (p. 402), and in another with a
"powerful emotion . . . on him, a childish one . . ." (p. 390).
Eddie's impotence with Bea speaks for itself.

Eddie's concern for his name is not a late development in
the play; nor is it evidence of split aims in *A View*. The story
about the boy who informed shows that the neighborhood,
of which Eddie is a part, lives by a certain code of self-respect.
When Bea complains of Eddie's sexual indifference to her, he
silences her and says: "I want my respect, Beatrice" (p. 426).
The more obvious instances here need no underlining.

Since Eddie fails to achieve "insight" the traditionalist has
little difficulty in dismissing Eddie as no "tragic hero." Miller,
who is partial to "traditional" criteria himself at times (witness
The Crucible) but who sees that there is often a discrepancy
between venerable theory and the conditions of modern life
(witness *Salesman*), has not falsified Eddie in order to fill a
conventional mold. Repeatedly, Eddie has the opportunity for
insight but fails to achieve perspective on his plight. Not even
the passionate kiss on Catherine's mouth opens his eyes. Is this
credible? Miller, let us own, had a problem; he had to create a

character who would go all the way, who would not quit in the middle, who would, if you like, "prove the theme" (in the good sense). Intelligent characters often (but of course not always) compromise; that is, they "settle for half" (Alfieri). Even the average person today knows something about Freud; once this self-consciousness is introduced in a play, vacillation, rumination, and excessive verbalization threatens; what we are likely to get then is either "drama of ideas" (in the bad sense) or case history, documentation, rather than dramatic action. Miller has avoided these errors. Given Eddie's character and the credibility of his development, the charge that his death is not organic but merely heroically conventional, seems perverse. It has also been objected that Eddie is boring—too stupid, in effect, to command our interest consistently for two acts. Granted that Eddie is not burdened with excessive intelligence, it remains a fair question, as I hope to show later, whether critics have appreciated the psychological complexity that is part of Eddie's character.

Bea is less complex than Eddie (or, for that matter, less complex than Catherine or Rodolpho). According to Eddie, his wife has a "heart" (p. 383), and Bea proves it in the course of the play. After Eddie has informed, for example, and after all the other characters, including his beloved Catherine, have turned against him, Bea's "final thrust is to turn toward him instead of running from him" (p. 431). Bea agrees not to attend Catherine's wedding because Eddie forbids it (p. 436). When Eddie dies, it is Bea who "covers him with her body" (p. 439). Earlier, when Catherine says that Eddie, because he has informed, belongs in the "garbage," Bea, against the logic of events, argues: "Then we all belong in the garbage . . . whatever happened we all done it. . . ." (p. 436). Bea has some fight in her, however; she actively opposes Eddie's neurotic fixation. First, she argues him into accepting the fact that Catherine must work; second, she wants to be "a wife again"

(p. 399); third, she tries to argue Catherine into maturity; fourth (the list is not exhaustive), even at the end, as Eddie steps out to meet his death, she cries:

> The truth is not as bad as blood, Eddie! I'm tellin' you the truth—tell her good-by forever! (p. 438)

Bea, then, is not precisely one-dimensional.

According to Eddie, Catherine is "the madonna type"; Rodolpho calls her "beautiful"; but Miller says nothing about her appearance. Catherine is seventeen; like most girls her age, she wants to dress in style, she wants to work and be independent, and she wants to get married. Catherine is a high school graduate and the best student in her stenography class (p. 384); nevertheless, she reads movie magazines (p. 411). Catherine is caught in a conflict between dependence on Eddie and her normal need for self-realization. Bea says: "you gotta be your own self more. You still think you're a little girl . . ." (p. 405). Although there is some evidence for a sexual attachment to Eddie (p. 421), the evidence is slight. When Bea criticizes the girl, Miller says that Catherine "is trying to rationalize a buried impulse" (p. 404); but, on the whole, this "impulse" would seem to be one of dependence, in view of the fact that Bea describes Catherine's attitude in terms of "baby," "little girl," and "twelve years old"; and Rodolpho refers to her as a "little bird" (p. 421). Catherine's "rationalization" is chiefly that she does not want to hurt Eddie (p. 404). There is a good deal of fight in Catherine, too; that is, her desire for self-realization is stronger than her wish to be dependent. Her fight for the right to work prepares us for her fight to possess Rodolpho. When Eddie injects suspicion about Rodolpho's motives into her this complicates the action (p. 419); but her love for the boy is stronger than her doubts; when Eddie kisses her she does not react, but when Eddie kisses Rodolpho she "tears at Eddie's face," threatens to "kill" him, and glares "at him in horror" (pp. 422-423). Her emancipation is properly gradual; for example, although she threatens to leave with Rodolpho, she does not immediately do so (p. 425). Eddie's kissing Rodolpho, which was calculated to stop the love affair, ironically becomes the means that incites Catherine more strongly against Eddie (p. 424). But the betrayal is the decisive event in this regard. "To hell with Eddie," says Catherine in the prison scene (p. 434). Yet traces of the old love remain to keep Catherine human and interesting. When she learns that Marco is coming to kill Eddie, for example, she pleads with Eddie to save himself (p. 436). Catherine, however, is not a very perceptive girl; even after Eddie's kiss she seems blind to his motives. When Bea, at the end, accuses Eddie of incestuous desires, Catherine is "horrified" (p. 437).

Rodolpho is Italian; but unlike Marco he has long blond hair ("A thousand years ago," he says, ". . . the Danes invaded Sicily" [p. 392]). This blond hair, made incongruous in the context of the play, becomes a symbol, it will be seen, of what some critics consider Rodolpho's "ambiguity." In order to do justice to Rodolpho's character, which is complex, it is necessary to compare what Rodolpho says about himself with what others say about him. The first time Rodolpho is seen he is impressed by the Carbone house (p. 391). Upstairs, Rodolpho says: "I have a nice face, but no money" (p. 394). Rodolpho's aim is to become rich (p. 394). He claims to have earned once enough money to live for six months (p. 395). He admits to a burning desire to see the bright lights of Times Square (p. 401). When Marco is coming to kill Eddie, Rodolpho confesses:

> It is my fault, Eddie. Everything. I wish to apologize. It was wrong that I do not ask your permission to court Catherine. (p. 437)

According to Eddie, Rodolpho's "nice face" is suspect. But

Catherine regards her lover as sufficiently masculine. Bea agrees
with the girl: "he's a kid; he don't know how to behave himself yet"; "He's a nice fella, hard workin' . . . good-lookin' . . ."
(p. 398). Before having seen Rodolpho, Alfieri is sceptical of
Eddie's evaluation (p. 424); after seeing Rodolpho, Alfieri says
nothing. Miller's description of the kissing incident and the
ensuing struggle has already been quoted. Some critics have
suggested that Eddie and Rodolpho are both suspect in sexual
terms; that is, that both men are possibly latent-homosexual.
Does anyone in the play view Rodolpho as Eddie does? This important question has not been asked by those critics who over-
emphasize this aspect of the play. Eddie says that the men
on the docks call Rodolpho "Paper Doll" and similar unflatter-
ing names (p. 398); Louis and Mike are introduced to confirm
this statement (pp. 400-401). Marco, who is accepted by the
workers because he meets certain stereotyped requirements of
"masculinity," thinks that the men laugh at his brother "because he's got a sense of humor . . . which he's got [says Eddie]
but that ain't what they're laughin'" (p. 408). In his introduction to the first edition of A View, Miller, in a lightly
sarcastic manner, said that the play has a "homosexual motif"
—but he did not say whether that "motif" has a real or an
imaginary basis in the drama. When Eddie punches Rodolpho
at the end of Act One, Miller writes:

> Rodolpho: No, no, he didn't hurt me. *To Eddie with a
> certain gleam and a smile:* I was only surprised. (p. 416)

One could, of course, make much of this; what, for instance,
is the meaning of "a certain gleam"? Does Miller intend a
knowing or hostile "gleam"? Or is something perverse (femi-
nine-masochistic) meant? To answer this and related questions,
it is necessary to view the play as a whole; consequently further
discussion along this line will have to wait until the discussion
of theme. As for Rodolpho's character in its general outline,

Marco claims that his brother exaggerates—for Rodolpho
earned enough money singing to live for two months, not six
(p. 395). Marco also accuses his brother of being a dreamer
(p. 395). Eddie puts this thought, however, in much stronger
terms:

> Is that a workin' man [he asks Catherine]? What does
> he do with his first money? A snappy new jacket he
> buys, records, a pointy pair of new shoes and his brother's
> kids are starvin' over there with tuberculosis? That's a
> hit-and-run guy, baby; he's got bright lights in his head,
> Broadway. Them guys don't think of nobody but their-
> self! (p. 403)

Eddie's motives aside, who refutes the charge? Eddie claims
that Rodolpho lacks "respect" because he fails to ask permission to court Catherine; and, at the end, as I have indicated,
Rodolpho admits as much. Moreover, a comparison of the two
versions of the play, which I shall take up later, will reveal
that in the final version Miller has reversed responsibility for
the seduction and made Rodolpho more nearly the initiator.
These people are Roman Catholics (p. 387), with strict views
on premarital sexual intercourse. Has Miller complicated the
action here by making Rodolpho less easily defined? Rodolpho
is an elusive character, one with an unknown factor about him
which stimulates the imagination and enhances our sense of
the "real." It is well to remember that no great character in
literature can be completely rationalized.

(Alfieri's position in the play is a special one, and it would
be best to wait a moment and consider the lawyer's role in
relation to the theme of the play.)

Marco is dark (p. 392); "he is a square-built peasant of
thirty-two, suspicious, tender, and quiet-voiced" (p. 391).
Marco is, in some respects, a foil to Rodolpho. Says Eddie:
"Marco goes around like a man; nobody kids Marco"

(p. 398). Marco is no dreamer—not with a wife and three children depending on him. Marco lives by a primitive code; he says (with Antigone): "All the law is not in a book" (p. 434). Before going off to kill Eddie, Marco prays in a church (p. 436). For Marco there is no incongruity here; for Eddie has violated a sacred code; more: "He degraded my brother. . . . He robbed my children, he mocks my work" (p. 434). Marco is well-motivated, then; we are prepared in advance for his destruction of Eddie. Nevertheless, Marco remains a rather flat character; he is much simpler than the other characters, including Bea; he is, moreover, a static character, for there is, in the course of the play, no basic alteration in his character. The same is true of Bea and Rodolpho (and Alfieri); they remain fundamentally unchanged by the events of the play. Not Eddie and Catherine, however; for both develop—Eddie's betrayal signals a major change in his person, while Catherine's revolt is similarly a decisive turn in her drive toward self-realization.

Although some critics have found, as was the case in *Salesman* and *Crucible*, a thematic "split" in *A View*, my detailed discussion of structure in the first section of this chapter should suggest the impossibility of separating the "incest theme" and the "betrayal theme"; in other words, the "personal" and the "social" are again integrated in Miller's play. Why invent problems where none exist? There are several minor themes richly coordinated in *A View*, but at the base of the structure is Eddie's love for Catherine, and this love is so intense, so powerful, that it drives Eddie to betray a sacred trust. The betrayal, then, is only a means to an end, namely, Eddie's passionate desire to retain Catherine. If Eddie had, in a jealous rage, murdered Catherine, or Rodolpho, or both, would there then have been a "split" between the "incest theme" and the "murder theme"? If, in his despair, Eddie had committed suicide, would there then have been a "split" between the "incest theme" and the "suicide theme"? (Is there a "split" between Othello's jealousy and his destruction of Desdemona?)

Nor is there any evidence in the play, as has been claimed, for economic *determinism*. Influence, yes; but Eddie was not forced to betray Rodolpho and Marco (he might have killed his rival—or even "settled for half"), but Eddie chose betrayal, it is well to remember, because that is the turn Miller wanted his character to take (that the turn involves social consequences does not conflict with the central thrust of the play), and as a playwright Miller's job was to make that turn credible —and in that he succeeded admirably. Even if it could be demonstrated that Marco acts out of economic necessity in his murderous attack on Eddie, one would not be wise to over-emphasize this aspect of the play because it would involve switching the focus from Eddie, who is clearly the protagonist, to Marco. There is, then, no evidence in the play for a one-sided deterministic interpretation. There is here, as in "real" life, an element of "mystery"; says Alfieri:

> It wasn't as though there was a mystery to unravel. I could see every step coming . . . I knew where he was heading for, I knew where he was going to end. (p. 410)

If so, then why does Alfieri repeatedly reason with Eddie? From one standpoint, Eddie seems determined; from another, the effect of the play depends on our sense that it all might have been otherwise (even as it does in *Othello*, which also deals with a jealous man).

A good deal of critical energy, as I have suggested, has also been expended on the question of the "homosexual motif" in *A View*. One must be cautious here. Miller seems to be contrasting the European and the American cultures. It has often been remarked that in the last war American soldiers tended to find the manners of European males, notably the expressive Latin types, "effeminate." Eddie and the other longshoremen find this "effeminate" quality in Rodolpho. But "effeminacy" (whether the European or American variety) is, as the psycho-analyst Edmund Bergler has shown, no reliable index to homo-sexuality. It might be argued that Eddie is reacting "culturally" toward Rodolpho; that he is shifting the guilt he feels, uncon-sciously, for his lust toward Catherine into the shape of homo-sexual accusations against Rodolpho ("It's not me but the other guy that's not right!"); that Eddie is just looking for any excuse to possess Catherine; that his kissing Rodolpho is merely a sign of contempt; that it is a symbolic castration of the boy in Catherine's presence; that it is a prefiguring Judas kiss of betrayal—in short, there are any number of explanations for the specific act. The evil of false accusation is that it creates an aura of guilt around the subject where in fact no guilt exists. (It is well to recall that Miller had recently completed *The Crucible* when he wrote *A View*.) Nevertheless, there is no way to "prove" that Eddie is *not* suffering (alone or in company with the other longshoremen) from latent-homosexuality (the same might be said for Rodolpho). Certainly the orthodox Freudian would maintain that this latency is often a feature of incestuous fixations; but art, to utter a cliché, is not life—and in terms of Miller's play as a whole the burden of proof would seem to rest with the accuser. But if, after all is said, the ambiguity remains—what of it? Miller is often accused of writing melo-dramatic sermons; but ambiguity suggests the complexity and concreteness of life itself. Are we always certain about people we meet? Is there not always an element of mystery, of am-biguity even (sexual and/or otherwise) in our encounters with others? Why should ambiguity, commonly lauded in other dramatists, be condemned in Miller?

The analysis of structure reveals that Alfieri is integrated into the action of the play. Aside from his role as a chorus-figure who comments on the action and bridges time lapses, Alfieri appears in several scenes as an actor. It is as a com-mentator, however, that he has been assailed. The crucial question, it would seem, is whether Alfieri's comments are superfluous. And in a strict sense, one might indeed argue that there is a certain redundancy here. In a broader sense, however —and the question is being restricted to his chorus role alone— the play would be much less rich in texture without him. Alfieri's comments clearly help to extend the scope of the action, and his speech is well-orchestrated with that of the other, less articulate, characters in the play.

Before considering the question of the final speech in A View, it might be well to recall some facts concerning the question of codes. Eddie will not accept as final the law that says he cannot stop Catherine from marrying Rodolpho. Nor will he accept, finally, that other code that says one must not betray a trust. When the first law fails, as Eddie sees it, he breaks the second law. Marco cannot understand a law that says Eddie cannot be punished for breaking the second law. Therefore, Marco violates the first law as justification and he kills Eddie. Neither man, then, can live within the limits of that law which Alfieri and all "civilized" men commit themselves to in greater or lesser degree. Both men, by transgressing that first code, however, destroy themselves—for Eddie was as willing to murder Marco as Marco was open to the destruction of Eddie.

Finally, Alfieri's verbal distinctions in his curtain speech would not seem to be irrelevant or illegitimate:

> Most of the time now we settle for half and I like it better. But the truth is holy, and even as I know how wrong he was and his death useless, I tremble, for I confess that something perversely pure calls to me from his memory—not purely good, but himself purely, for he allowed himself to be wholly known and for that I think I will love him more than all my sensible clients. And yet, it is better to settle for half, it must be! And so I mourn him—I admit it—with a certain . . . alarm.
> (p. 439)

It is certainly valid to discriminate between the act and the agent; that is, "not purely good" (the act was "bad") but "himself purely" (the uninhibited expression of himself). Eddie "allowed himself to be wholly known"—but "wholly known" to *others*, obviously, and not, as it has sometimes been claimed, "wholly known" to himself (which would be patently false). It should also be obvious that Alfieri intends that "the truth is holy" to *him* (that is, to Alfieri) and "holy" *in itself*, but certainly not "holy" to Eddie, who has consistently resisted the truth. Nor does it seem that we are asked to discriminate, as some critics contend, between Eddie's psychological problem and his social transgression; it is all of a piece in this respect: "I know how wrong he was, and his death useless . . ." would not appear to erect any distinctions; nor does Alfieri—or Miller —ask for forgiveness of Eddie. We are asked, it would seem, to understand. (It is possible that for some readers, to understand all is to forgive all—but that is another matter.) Furthermore, we are not asked to admire Eddie; but we are asked, it seems, to respond to his fate with a certain awe—for, in a sense, Eddie has acted out impulses which, so the psychoanalysts inform us, we all share but which most of us manage to repress or renounce or sublimate. In like manner, the Christian moralist will stress that all of us have been guilty, at one time or another, of betraying God, and beside this, Eddie's transgression might be seen in its true proportion. There would seem to be, then, a simple but powerful resonance in Miller's play.

A Note on the Two Versions of
A View from the Bridge

This Note is not intended as an exhaustive comparison of both texts; only certain significant changes will be noted— changes which I believe aid in interpreting the final version; moreover, for some changes not considered here Miller has himself supplied the commentary. (See the "Introduction" to the *Collected Plays* and also the "Note" to the original edition of *A View*. Although Miller's critical reflections are extremely interesting, there is space here for only a few observations. In the "Note," Miller argues for a simple line of development uncluttered by "antecedent life forces"; "I am tired of documentation," says Miller, "which, while perfectly apt and evidently reasonable, does not add anything to our comprehension of the tale's essence" (pp. 16-17). Miller is, of course, attacking the device of character traits here. Traits that make no contribution to action and/or theme—and what is "essence" here but action and/or theme?—deserve censure; but in Miller's best work, as I have tried to show, his "documentation" is not inessential. Traits are necessary and background is called for when credibility would suffer without them. Eddie Carbone's fate is credible without recourse to many traits or extensive background drawing. There would seem to be no reason to disparage one valid approach in order to justify another equally legitimate mode of characterization. Also worthy of note are Miller's thoughts on the expanded cast in the London production. The text suggests social extension through a few representative neighborhood characters; but in the London production many more characters were placed on stage, and Miller regards this larger cast as a definite gain in depth and comprehensiveness. Miller may very well be correct in his view—one must never underrate the force of a theatrical image. Yet even in the final text the presence of the two extra aliens and their relatives seem to add nothing to the play that is not sufficiently clear from figures such as Marco, Rodolpho, Louis, and Mike. Present here, in a somewhat altered fashion, I think, is the fallacy of *All My Sons*, in which the multiplication of actors appeared to be designed for increased social relevance. The fallacy reappears in an extremely destructive fashion in *After the Fall*. Perhaps Miller tends to undervalue the power of symbolization and representation. Finally, Miller's

belief in the simplicity of Eddie is somewhat misleading, for
my analysis suggests that Eddie is more complex than his creator
—and some critics—allow.)

In the original version of *A View*, at the end of Act One,
when Eddie strikes Rodolpho, Miller says:

> Rodolpho, *as a new song comes on the radio, his voice
> betraying a new note of command*: Dance, Catherine.
> Come. (p. 129)

In the final version there is no reference to "a new note of
command." Why not? Is it a small matter? As I shall try to
suggest, it is part of an effort to make Rodolpho more complex.
The commanding gesture indicates sufficient masculinity on
Rodolpho's part; it tends to clarify that "certain gleam" mentioned earlier; the final version is less certain here. In Act Two
of the first version, Catherine is the seducer:

> Catherine: Now. There's nobody here.
> Rodolpho: Oh, my little girl. Oh God!
> Catherine, *kissing his face:* Now!
> (p. 136)

Here is the second version:

> Catherine, *softly:* Hold me.
> Rodolpho, *clasping her to him:* Oh, my little girl.
> Catherine: Teach me. *She is weeping.* I don't know any-
> thing, teach me, Rodolpho, hold me.
> Rodolpho: There's nobody here now. Come inside.
> Come.
> (p. 421)

Although the change may seem to make Rodolpho more masculine in the second version, the chief concern, I suggest, is to

place the responsibility more nearly on the boy. The final effect is to win more sympathy for Eddie at the expense of Rodolpho. Eddie appears on the scene after the above; in the first version he touches a hot iron and tells Catherine: "You start a fire that way." This is fine irony. Why was it cut from the second version? The pattern of paper that replaced it, I have argued, is a symbol of "Paper Doll"; here, in the final version, it more nearly keeps Rodolpho's "ambiguity" before us—thus, quite possibly, gaining sympathy for Eddie; that is, if Rodolpho "ain't right" then perhaps, somehow, Eddie is less "wrong." Note that in the final version Eddie says: "Rodolpho makin' you a dress?"—again this sarcasm keeps the problem of Rodolpho in the air to vex us. This bid for increased sympathy for Eddie in the final version (*not* "admiration," nor *necessarily* "forgiveness") can be seen in the fact that originally Eddie kisses Catherine "on the lips" and speaks "like a lover" *twice*; the second time occurs near the climax of the play (pp. 157-158). The removal of this physical and, finally, repulsive aspect of Eddie's love to one manifestation succeeds perhaps in making that love a bit less unacceptable to us. The irony that closes the final version just before Alfieri's speech is absent from the original, in which Eddie dies asking "Why?" —and that is all (p. 159). Alfieri's final speech has been altered too:

> Most of the time now we settle for half,
> And I like it better.
> And yet, when the tide is right
> And the green smell of the sea
> Floats in through my window,
> The waves of this bay
> Are the waves against Siracusa,
> And I see a face that suddenly seems carved;
> The eyes look like tunnels

Leading back toward some ancestral beach
Where all of us once lived.

And I wonder at those times
How much of all of us
Really lives there yet,
And when we truly have moved on,
On and away from that dark place,
That world that has fallen to stones?
(pp. 159-160)

Does this speech, as someone has claimed, make Eddie guilty,
whereas the later one exonerates him? Admittedly, the second
version renders Eddie more sympathetic; but neither version,
I think, makes Eddie "guiltless."

CHAPTER SIX

After the Fall

For six years after *A View from the Bridge* was first produced in New York, no new Miller play appeared before the public. It was rumored that during his absence from Broadway, Miller had written four or five plays but that none of them had satisfied him. Miller did unveil, however, a film called *The Misfits* (1961), which was subsequently published as a "cinema-novel" (a "Note" on this work will appear at the end of the present chapter). Finally, when many observers of the theater scene were perhaps prepared to declare that Miller would write no more plays, *After the Fall* (1964), a long two-act drama, was presented as the première production of the Lincoln Center Repertory Company in New York City.

In the scope and seriousness of the themes involved, in sheer bulk and number of characters, perhaps even in technique, *After the Fall* is Miller's most ambitious work. The play is designed for an open stage—a stage without curtains, proscenium arch, or scenery. "The action," says Miller, "takes place in the mind, thought, and memory of Quentin" (p. 1). Quentin is a "successful" New York lawyer who has reached what some would call a spiritual impasse, others an existential crisis, and still others simply a neurotic collapse (perhaps the categories are not mutually exclusive). A chair downstage facing "front, toward the audience" "holds" the Listener, "who, if he could be seen, would be sitting just beyond the edge of the stage itself" (p. 2). In a monologue, interspersed with dramatic episodes that enact the verbalizations, Quentin tells the Listener the story of his life. Says Miller: "The 'Listener,' who to some will be a psychoanalyst, to others God, is Quentin himself turned at the edge of the abyss to look at his experiences, his nature and his time. . . ." (*Saturday Evening Post*, February 1, 1964). The stage directions, then, are highly relevant:

> The setting consists of three levels rising to the highest at the back, crossing in a curve from one side of the stage to the other. A stairway, center, connects them. Rising above all, and dominating the stage, is the blasted stone tower of a German concentration camp. Its wide lookout windows are like eyes which at the moment seem blind and dark; bent reinforcing rods stick out of it like broken tentacles. On the two lower levels are sculpted areas; indeed, the whole effect is neolithic, a lava-like, supple geography in which, like pits and hollows found in lava, the scenes take place. The mind has no color but its memories are brilliant against the grayness of its landscape. When people sit they do so on any of the abutments, ledges, or crevices. A scene may start in a confined area, but spread or burst out onto the entire stage, overrunning any other area.
>
> People appear and disappear instantaneously, as in the mind; but it is not necessary that they walk off the stage. The dialogue will make clear who is "alive" at any moment and who is in abeyance. The effect, therefore, will be the surging, flitting, instantaneousness of a mind questing over its own surfaces and into its depths. (p. 1)

The mode of imitation in *Fall*, it need hardly be added, is non-representational. The point of view is wholly Quentin's. Typically, Quentin bridges the scenes from his past by addressing the Listener, and quite often during a scene he delivers remarks to the empty chair in the manner of an aside. Telephones and other props are usually described in the text as "invisible" (see, for example, p. 18). The scenes that take place when Quentin is a boy are played to an invisible and silent Quentin. Techniques from the cinema are freely employed; for instance, in one scene a character "vanishes as the tower appears" (p. 34), a device which is similar to the rapid replacement and juxtaposition of images on the screen where analogies and contrasts are underlined. Sound effects are also used imaginatively; the roar of a jet plane accompanies one character's arrival at an "airport" (p. 68); the screech of a subway car helps to remind Quentin that his best friend committed suicide by jumping under the wheels of a train (p. 111). Symbolic methods which owe nothing to any other medium are used, too. In several scenes, "anonymous men appear" around Quentin and the heroine, and these shadowy figures are visual projections that suggest the nameless men in the heroine's past, as well as in her present (p. 49). Miller also indulges in what he calls "condensed dialogue," a technique calculated to create the impression of "time swiftly passing in the mind." Thus, Quentin and his second wife are listening to a recording she has made and the latter is unhappy with her pianist. Suddenly Quentin steps out of the scene and shouts:

> Weinstein, get her Johnny Black!
> *The music turns over into another number and her voice, swift, sure.*
> There now! Listen now!
> (p. 101)

Note that the dialogue is not "condensed" in the sense that the language itself is truncated or mutilated; perhaps it would be more correct to say that time is condensed, which, in turn, results in a condensation of speech. Characters, as the stage directions suggest, come and go by the "logic" of the free association of ideas. In structural terms, the rapid appearance and disappearance of certain characters is, in part, a device for foreshadowing, a means of suggesting complications and arousing suspense. In thematic terms, the characters are, in part, recurring motifs. Enough has been said, perhaps, to suggest the special techniques of the play and the aura in which the action unfolds. It is time to look at the action itself.

Out of the semi-darkness that covers the stage, which only partially reveals figures moving about and whispering in a seemingly aimless manner, steps Quentin downstage to confront the audience and address the Listener. Apparently Quentin and the Listener are old acquaintances. After a few pleasantries, Quentin states his reason for calling the Listener:

> I have a bit of a decision to make. You know—you mill around about something for months and all of a sudden there it is and you're at a loss for what to do. Were you able to give me two hours? It might not take that long [it takes three hours], but I think it involves a great deal and I'd rather not rush. (p. 2)

Quentin's "decision" is whether, after two broken marriages, he has the right to take on the burden of a third. Actually, however, "it involves a great deal" more than this, for the "decision" does not pose itself in isolation from Quentin's total experience. What emerges, finally, is Quentin's attempt to find the source of his failure in love by tracking that failure to what he believes to be its lair in the dark past, but, not content with psychoanalysis alone, Quentin seeks to relate this private drama to a wider field of causation, of social and cultural and historical experience, in such a manner that what appears to be Quentin's unique experience is in reality the essential journey of Everyman through the modern world.

Act One may be viewed as chiefly a vehicle for conveying

the basic background of Quentin that will enable us to grasp the significance of the failure attending his second marriage in Act Two, which in many respects is the dramatic core of the play, and to prepare us for the final insights which close the play. Immediately, Quentin establishes his present circumstances. About fourteen months back, Quentin explains, a few weeks after his second wife, Maggie, died, he quit his lucrative law practice because it had "lost its necessity" (p. 2). About ten months later, around the time that his mother died, Quentin met Holga, a German archaeologist. His indecision in respect to marrying Holga is not simply doubt about his ability to love; it also involves the question of life's meaning:

> I think now that my disaster really began when I looked up one day . . . and the bench was empty. No judge in sight. And all that remained was the endless argument with oneself, this pointless litigation of existence before an empty bench. (p. 3)

Holga, however, is a source of "hope" to Quentin: "if I could corner that hope," he says, "find what it consists of and either kill it for a lie, or really make it mine . . ." (p. 4). Thus, in the first two and a half pages of monologue, Miller establishes the point of attack—Quentin has reached a turning point in his life, he is faced with a decision that must alter the circumstances of his life, and the major dramatic questions have been framed.

For the sake of clarity and brevity, it would seem wise to isolate the various movements, or "associations," of action in the play and to present them in a coherent order, remembering, however, that these summaries are translations from what are in the play most often not continuous developments but fragmentary episodes that violate chronology. In view of the fact that *Fall* stresses Quentin's character to an unusually high degree, for Miller, and heavily emphasizes theme, much will be

left out of account here that can be treated with more profit
elsewhere.

A number of structural developments may be isolated in Act
One: first, there is Quentin's relationship to his parents; second,
there is Quentin's sexual relationships—with his first wife,
Louise, with the girl who becomes his second wife in Act Two,
Maggie, with a casual acquaintance, Felice, and, finally, with
Holga; and lastly, there is Quentin's relationship with his
friends—Lou, Elsie, and Mickey—who link the other two
strands of action to a wider social reference. These three movements converge toward a connection in Quentin's mind with
the Nazi concentration camp, partly by the experiences of
Holga, who had survived one of the camps.

Quentin's mother married Quentin's father because her parents arranged the match for her. In spite of this, the girl had
been impressed by her fiance's appearance. Unhappily, this
romantic view soon disappeared when the young wife discovered
that her husband could neither read nor write. What made
this discovery particularly painful to the girl was the fact that
she had given up her plans to go to college in order to marry
in deference to her parents' wishes. In her disappointment, she
turned to Quentin, vowing that *he* would learn to read and
write beautifully (pp. 19-20). When the economic crash came
in 1929, Quentin's father, like many others, lost his money.
The mother calls her husband, at this point, a "moron" and
an "idiot," convinced that her mate has bungled away the
business (p. 22). At the mother's death, however, the father
is broken with grief; but Quentin cynically observes that in
spite of the loss, his father managed to vote in the next election (p. 11). In spite of his cynicism, guilt haunts Quentin, for
he cannot grieve over his mother's death (p. 7) and he feels,
moreover, a vague link between the mother-son alliance against
the father and the Nazi tower across the sea (p. 23).

Quentin's marriage with Louise is as unsatisfactory as was
the marriage of his parents. Louise, in fact, believes that there

is a causal connection between the two marriages, in the sense that Quentin is influenced too much by his mother; says Louise: "you don't really see any woman. Except in some ways your mother" (p. 32). Quentin, in this view, has been fashioned by his mother into a selfish man. On Quentin's side, the fault, he feels, is partly Louise's, inasmuch as he finds his wife cold in bed (p. 45). Quentin admits to having slept with another woman once, but he did it, he says, because Louise had threatened to divorce him (p. 45). Louise refuses to play the adoring mother-role any longer to what she conceives to be Quentin's childish megalomania; she wants to be loved and appreciated as a separate person (p. 46). When she discovers that Quentin has passed time with Maggie, she refuses to sleep with him any longer (p. 63). Three years later, Quentin relates, the marriage ended (p. 67).

Maggie is presented as an uneducated girl who has suffered from being unloved as a child (pp. 78-79). She has sought to compensate for this inner emptiness by a series of superficial sexual affairs (p. 89). Quentin assumes a protective stance toward Maggie (at least that is what he convinces himself it is at first [p. 91]); but even in the beginning he is strangely attracted to the girl, to her naive openness to experience, to her ability to live fully and sensuously in the present moment (p. 86), a trait far different from his own excessively cerebral and cautious approach to life.

Little need be said about Felice, who means "nothing" to Quentin (p. 7), and who appears to be merely someone to cling to for a time between Maggie's death and the encounter with Holga. Quentin had arranged Felice's divorce and subsequently became friendly with her, seemingly taking an interest in her hopes and plans for the future, and, in short, eliciting the girl's admiration for his concern. As far as Felice is aware, Quentin refutes Louise's charge that he is wholly self-absorbed, but on Quentin's side there is self-doubt about the authenticity of his role (pp. 4-7).

Holga is drawn to Quentin partly because she shares his increasing sense of guilt and complicity with evil. Holga, who
survived Hitler's era, declares: "no one they didn't kill can be
innocent again" (p. 23). For Quentin, Holga promises a way
of overcoming the paralysis of will from which he suffers because she is convinced that, in spite of the evil in life, "one
must finally take one's life in one's arms" (p. 24). Taking
Holga in his arms, then, is more than merely a sexual gesture
on Quentin's part.

The third strand of action in Act One involves Quentin's ex-
law professor, Lou. It was Lou's lies about Stalin's Russia, lies
from motives of mistaken loyalty to the goal of ultimate "per-
fection," that first disillusioned Quentin about his own sense
of innocence (p. 28). Lou is burdened with a wife, Elsie, who,
in addition to being a dominating shrew, would betray her mate
sexually with his best friend, Quentin (pp. 25-26). When Lou
is subpoenaed to appear before an investigating committee to
answer charges about his leftist activities in the Thirties, and
when another friend, Mickey, who is also subpoenaed, urges
Lou to "name names" with him (p. 40), the sensitive Lou is
emotionally overwhelmed and destroys himself under the wheels
of a subway train (p. 54).

In Act Two, Quentin's father seeks to rebuild his business,
and he asks his sons to help him. Dan, Quentin's older brother,
agrees to surrender his own plans for college and to stay behind
with the father, but Quentin, prodded by his mother, refuses
to sacrifice himself and departs instead for law school (pp. 73-
74). Near the end of the play, in a crucial and partly hallucina-
tory scene, a scene which depicts the final collapse of Quentin's
second marriage, there is made concrete and projected Quentin's hatred for his mother, stemming largely from an incident
out of his childhood when the mother had deceived her boy
and left him behind with a nurse while she went to Atlantic
City with her husband. In the scene with Maggie, Quentin,

confused with rage, suddenly finds himself torn by unconscious eruptions from his past and, instead of facing his wife, he is confronted by his mother—whom he proceeds to choke in a murderous frenzy (p. 125).

The main action of the second act, however, involves the relationship between Quentin and Maggie. One might locate the turning point of the play in the wedding scene between Quentin and Maggie, which occurs about midway in the act (pp. 99-100), in view of the fact that this moment marks the highest level perhaps of Quentin's fatal ignorance about himself, and it is the point from which Quentin's descent into his final crisis really gathers force. Due to the particular form of the play, however, such designations are not especially meaningful and seem a bit arbitrary. Maggie, who in Act Two has become a famous popular singer, grows increasingly dependent on alcohol and sleeping pills, and, in her neurotic insecurity, which was foreshadowed in the first act, she strikes out against everyone, not least of all Quentin. Like Louise, Maggie now accuses Quentin of being "cold" (p. 102), but in addition, she charges him with not working hard enough for her rights (p. 104). Quentin grows more and more dissatisfied, not only with Maggie, but also with himself. He begins to believe that perhaps he does *not* know how to love, that he has been more guilty of evil than he has been willing to allow. Yet Quentin refuses to assume *all* the responsibility; he insists that others—Louise, Maggie, his mother, everyone—share the guilt of hatred and, because the Nazis were part of humanity, even murder (p. 127). The climax of the play occurs when Maggie, who has had a bitter argument with Quentin, swallows a number of sleeping pills in an effort to shift the guilt for her self-destruction onto Quentin. The latter, enraged, reaches for Maggie. This is the moment in which Quentin has a fantasy of choking his mother. When the "superimposed shot" (to borrow a filmic term) concerning the mother disappears, Quentin finds himself strangling his wife; before regaining his senses, he presses Maggie into unconsciousness (p. 126). This is perhaps the crisis of the play. With this, the marriage ends and, a few months later, as Quentin tells it, Maggie fulfills her suicide threat (p. 126).

The play ends, as it began, on a two and a half page monologue. Quentin, in effect, summarizes the theme of the play in the guise of his final insights. He owns that he had tried to kill Maggie, and he accepts—in a manner that suggests a climax—the responsibility for that deed. Within the stretching shadow of the Nazi tower, however, Quentin insists again that his guilt is not an isolated thing, and that his relief at being alive is a feeling shared by the survivors of the last war. A good thing would seem to have emerged from Quentin's experience, it seems, for now there is knowledge on his part of good and evil; now he knows that:

> the wish to kill is never killed, but with some gift of courage one may look into its face when it appears, and with a stroke of love . . . forgive it; again and again . . . forever? . . . No, it's not certainty. . . . But it does seem feasible . . . not to be afraid. Perhaps it's all one has. I'll tell [Holga] that . . . (p. 128)

Then, striding upward toward Holga, and leaving behind the figures from his buried life, Quentin hopefully embraces a new life as . . . "darkness takes them all" (p. 129).

Structural analysis of *After the Fall* reveals that a faulty point of view traps Miller into "saying" everything, or nearly everything of importance, twice—once in monologue directed to the Listener and once in enactment. A typical example is the scene immediately following the introductory monologue of the play. Felice emerges from the shadows of the open stage and there is an encounter between her and Quentin which consumes about three pages of text (pp. 4-7). The gist of the scene

is summarized by Quentin to the Listener, however, shortly
after the scene begins: "It's this: somehow, whatever I look at
I seem to see its death" (p. 4). Aside from the fact that this
idea of death-in-life was suggested in the introduction, the
scene is presented as little more than an illustrated sermon, or
as Quentin himself calls it, an "instance" (p. 4). The method,
then, seems not only repetitious but excessively abstract and
didactic. Exposition is often conveyed in solid blocks. There is,
of course, a natural tendency for this to happen whenever
Quentin talks for any length of time to the Listener; but it
also appears on occasion in the dramatic sequences—several of
Holga's expository speeches are to the point here (ten lines, p.
12; eleven lines, p. 13; eighteen lines, p. 16; and twenty-two
lines, p. 24). Foreshadowing is often a transparent device for
creating expectation and suspense. Early in the play, during a
scene between Quentin and Holga, an image of Maggie suddenly appears; says Quentin: "Maybe I can get to it later. I
can't now . . ." (p. 12). At the end of Act One, Maggie's
image once again appears before Quentin, and Quentin says:
"I'll get to it, honey . . . I'll get to it" (p. 68). Similarly, complications are often suggested in an awkward manner. After a
quarrel with Louise, Quentin says:

> Good God, can there be more? Can there be worse?
> *Turning to the Listener:*
> See, that's what's incredible to me—three years more!
> (p. 67)

There is almost no irony in the play, and what there is, is
heavyhanded. Elsie, who had tried to seduce Quentin, is the
subject of the following discourse:

> Louise: And you know how she admires you.
> *Quentin nods seriously. Suddenly he turns out* [sic] *the*

Listener and bursts into an agonized, ironical laughter.
He abruptly breaks it off, and returns to silence before
Louise. (p. 32)

The irony here would seem to speak for itself.

At first glance, the rapid "cutting" (Miller's play encourages
the use of filmic terms) from one character or scene to another
suggests complexity; in the final effect, however, the shifting
most often results, and this is especially true of Act One, not
in depth but in superficiality. In Act One, there is no discernible
line of steadily rising tension; action, instead of rising, circles
statically between monologue and "instance." Act Two is much
better in this respect, with its fairly steady focus on the dis-
integration of Quentin's second marriage, and with its painful
dramatic climax in Quentin's attempted murder of Maggie.
The play as a whole, however, fails to maintain rising tension.
One reason for this perhaps is that when the play opens
Quentin is very close to the insight he achieves when the play
ends—one hundred and twenty-nine pages, or three hours in
the theater, later. The chief difficulty, though, lies in the
nature of Miller's subject and in the point of view he has
chosen.

As a way of approaching this problem, it might be illustrative
to comment on the ending of Act One. Quentin must pause
in his recitation in order to allow the audience time to stretch
their legs. Given the subject matter and method of the play,
it is extremely difficult to accomplish this feat with any degree
of smoothness. Thus, Quentin agonizes one moment over the
mutations of human love—and in the next moment, he sends
the Listener to the toilet (p. 68). No doubt there is some irony
here, but the reader must judge for himself about its success.
Compare this ending in its technical awkwardness, its abrupt
change in tone, its flimsy motivation, and its crude foreshadowing ("I'll get to it, honey") with the brilliant closing of Act One
in *Death of a Salesman*. Why, if the Listener is "Quentin him-

self," must he be there on stage? When Act Two commences, Quentin remains alone for a moment; there then follows a scene between Quentin and Holga, and then a scene between Quentin and Louise, before the Listener returns. Although Quentin does not philosophize in the Listener's absence, one might fairly ask, Why not? Addressing the audience directly, without the device of the Listener, may or may not have been more theatrically engaging; I for one feel, and for reasons to be discussed in a moment, that its effect would be negligible. In either mode, for example, the conclusion of Act One would be difficult to render in a credible manner. The problem is complex.

"The action," it will be recalled, "takes place in the mind, thought, and memory of Quentin." From the beginning of the play, then, the audience is supposed to be locked as tightly inside Quentin's skull as the novel reader is locked inside the skull of Joyce's Bloom in the relevant section of *Ulysses*, or inside the skull of another Quentin in Faulkner's *The Sound and the Fury*. Joyce and Faulkner were scrupulously consistent in their method. Is Miller consistent in *Fall*? To repeat, the play is supposed to take place *inside* Quentin's mind. The stage levels are intended to represent various levels of Quentin's consciousness, and the figures moving in the darkness of the stage are mental representations of persons that Quentin has known. This is Miller's convention, and the reader should have no difficulty accepting it. Suddenly, however, one of the mental representations *inside* Quentin's skull disengages itself from the other mental representations and moves to the forestage. This is Quentin. Where, one might inquire, are we now? The second problem involves the Listener. Is "he" *inside* Quentin's skull? Apparently not—otherwise, why would Quentin trouble to bring "him" up to date on events? How can the Listener, except in a very loose figurative sense, be "Quentin himself" in view of the conclusion to Act One? The stage directions are misleading then—all the action does not take place inside Quentin's head. The Listener is evidently outside Quentin's head; and the scenes and visions, which in the absence of the Listener might be accepted as events inside Quentin's head, now seem to lack a warrant. In itself the confusion here is not necessarily ruinous. One might, for example, discount Miller's remarks about the Listener as Quentin and view the dummy simply as a sounding board or analyst. Or one might contend that an illogical convention is acceptable if the practical results are worth the concession. In the case of *Fall*, however, the presence of the Listener, whatever the rationale behind the device, would seem to have misled Miller, as I have said, into repetition. No doubt Miller felt that he required the Listener as an aid to selection; but an audience that can accept the convention of being inside a man's head as he stands before them and as action unfolds around him, can also accept the processes of a mind more ordered and focused than they would be in "real" life. In short, Miller could have dispensed with the Listener entirely and written, in my opinion, a more logical and more tightly constructed play.

In *After the Fall*, Miller has revived some of the techniques that he exploited successfully in *Death of a Salesman*. In the earlier play, Miller moved easily in and out of Willy Loman's mind, dissolved the barriers of time and place, and succeeded in recreating—"subjectively," "objectively," and "subjectively-objectively"—the significant moments in Willy's life. In *Fall*, time and place barriers are also erased and a life-story is compressed into two acts, but instead of an inarticulate salesman the focus is on a sophisticated lawyer. I have said that there is little or no irony in *Fall*. The irony in *Salesman* arose from the tension or interplay between appearance and reality, or between the three kinds of viewpoint. There is no such cross reference—hence no such tension—in *Fall*. A brief comparison of the play to the novel form may help to clarify the matter. It is generally agreed that in the novel the first person point of view is best if the focus of interest is on characters and events other than

the narrator. For one thing, it is very difficult for "I" to be
candid about himself. When, moreover, there is a strong philosophical bias in the first person narrative the reader is more
conscious than is usually the case that he is being urged to
evaluate the evidence solely on "I's" word for it. True, there
is concentration, unity, and a certain primitive veracity in the
mode ("I was there!"); but it remains, in terms of the reader's
immediate response, a more limited philosophical vision than
other modes of narrative, such as, the third person main character angle as developed chiefly by Henry James and refined
still further by Joyce, or even the older omniscient viewpoint
where the novelist, say Tolstoy, moved inside and outside his
characters at will. The difficulty for the reader of the stream of
consciousness novel, and it is well to recall that the total stream
of consciousness novel has been abandoned by writers, is
partially overcome by the fact that the reader can stop to puzzle
over a section. A play, however, demands immediate clarity.
Perhaps not even the "dream plays" of Strindberg are eminently
suitable for the stage. *Death of a Salesman* may be as far as
one can go in the direction of subjectivity, broken chronology,
and the like, on the stage; and Miller himself has said in
his "Introduction" to the *Collected Plays* why the *Salesman*
method could not be repeated:

> It is not possible, in my opinion, to graft it onto a char-
> acter whose psychology it does not reflect, and I have
> not used it since because it would be false to a more
> integrated—or less disintegrating—personality. . . . (p.
> 26)

Evidently the straightforward naturalistic method also seemed
unacceptable to Miller. (It is interesting to note that Eugene
O'Neill, after his experimental phase, returned to the naturalistic mode for his autobiographical play, *Long Day's Journey
Into Night*.)

Finally, the loose structure of *After the Fall* encourages abstract generalizations that do not always seem to spring naturally from concrete particulars, and, as I shall argue later, the form actually seems at odds with the main thrust of the play. Basically, Miller was much more critical of Willy Loman than he is of Quentin, and this critical attitude toward Willy permitted Miller to be ironic and to objectify part of Willy's story. This balance, as has been said, is missing from the later work. The reader stays confined with Quentin for a long time. Consequently, with no recourse to the objective, with no relief or contrast, the *character* of Quentin, the quality of his mind, even his speech, becomes exceedingly important.

The rationale for using the stream of consciousness as subject matter rests on the claim that it enables both writer and reader to come to closer grips with the complexities of character and that it reflects a more accurate picture of "real" life. Miller has taken pains to project Quentin—his past in terms of psychology, the conditioning forces of economic imperatives, and the influence on him of political ideologies. All of these factors are, to one degree or another, brought to bear on the protagonist in an effort to make Quentin not only an articulate man but a representative one as well. Although Miller, in his *Post* article, has said that his play "does not look toward social or political ideas as the creators of violence, but into the nature of the human being himself," this should not be interpreted to mean that there are no "social" or "political ideas" in the play. Once again, in order to appreciate what Miller has accomplished, it is desirable, at the risk perhaps of a certain minimum of repetition, to rearrange the facts concerning Quentin which are conveyed in a disjointed fashion in the play into a chronological and coherent pattern of development.

Quentin's character, Miller suggests, was partly determined inside his mother's womb:

The first time I felt you move [says Quentin's mother],

> I was standing on the beach at Rockaway. . . . And I
> saw a star, and it got bright, and brighter, and brighter!
> And suddenly it fell, like some great man had died, and
> you were being pulled out of me to take his place, and
> be a light, a light in the world! (p. 73)

The "great man" who "died" was Quentin's father, who remained, except in his wife's affections, very much alive. No
sexual motive between mother and son is ever stated or suggested; the play avoids an orthodox Freudian interpretation. At
the time of the economic crash, the mother finally verbalized
her intense dissatisfaction with her husband, and this harsh
articulation profoundly shocked the boy Quentin (pp. 22-23).
To Quentin the man, there was a "complicity" in evil in his
alliance with his mother against his father, a complicity not
unlike the one that all men, according to Quentin, share with
the Nazis (p. 23). Quentin was so outraged when his mother
left him behind on her trip to Atlantic City that upon her
return he attempted, or at least threatened, to kill himself (p.
84). That Quentin's hostility was primarily directed against his
mother rather than himself is clear from the scene described
above when Quentin chokes his mother. "A suicide kills two
people, Maggie," Quentin says at one point, "That's what it's
for" (p. 116). According to Quentin his mother was to blame
for dividing him from his father; but he refuses to generalize
and "lay it all to mothers" (p. 34). Quentin's attitude toward
his mother is an ambivalent one. He says:

> so many of my thoughts of [mother] degenerate into
> some crime; the truth is she was a light to me whenever
> it was dark. I loved that nut, and only love does make
> her real and mine. (p. 95)

In seven years of married life, Quentin and Louise apparently
never had a real "meeting" (p. 30). According to Louise, Quen-

tin has been spoiled by his mother. For example, Quentin admits that once he had wanted to be unfaithful to Louise but that he had desisted because: "I realized what you meant to me"; but Louise, far from being flattered, regards this confession as an effort on Quentin's part to cast her in the role of his mother, who used to beam at her son's "conquests" (pp. 32-33). As for his actual infidelity, perhaps Louise would never have learned of this affair if Quentin had not written a letter to the girl which Louise was permitted to discover. Quentin suggests that he "left that letter for [Louise] to read . . . in order to . . . somehow join the condemned . . . to start being real" (p. 60). The first time that Quentin encountered Maggie he had rushed home to inform Louise that he had wanted to sleep with the girl but that he "didn't because I thought of you, and in a new way . . . like a stranger I had never gotten to know" (p. 62). Louise also fails to appreciate the implications of this "compliment." She is persuaded that Quentin wants an end to their marriage, but that he lacks the courage to admit it (p. 61). Quentin's thought on the matter is expressed by an exclamation followed by what seems like a rhetorical question: "God! Can that be true?" (p. 63). Actually, to his way of thinking, Quentin has been abused, for he had tried to tell Louise the truth and he had received no thanks for it. Perhaps, he concludes, it would be best, more prudent, to "pursue Louise not with truth but with attention" (p. 67). Feelings of guilt, evidently inexplicable to Quentin, continue to plague him, however; thus he tells Holga:

> there were times when [Louise] looked into the mirror and I saw she didn't like her face, and I wanted to step between her and what she saw. I felt guilty even for her face! (p. 72)

Quentin's first impression of Maggie was that she was "silly" and "stupid," but he liked the fact that "she was just *there*,

like a tree or a cat" (p. 61). Admittedly, his feelings were, from
the start, mixed about her. He felt that she was a "joke," yet
he perceived in her "a strange, surprising honor" (pp. 78-79).
She offered Quentin not "power" alone—but also "salvation"
(p. 75). Quentin tells Maggie: "You're not pretending to be . . .
innocent!" (p. 82); and this fact is important to Quentin because Maggie represents "now" to him, whereas Louise is the
"future"—a "vase that must never be dropped" (p. 86). Later
Quentin admits that he had played the "cheap benefactor" with
Maggie (p. 79); that he could not sleep with her "without a
principle," and that the "principle" was "that she had to be
'saved' " (p. 91). The marriage between Quentin and Maggie
was a good one at first. Quentin gave himself freely, as he saw it,
of his time and labor to further Maggie's career; he says:

> Well, honey, I'm putting in forty per cent of my time on
> your problems . . . Maggie, I keep a log; I know what I
> spend my time on! (p. 104)

But Maggie's neuroticism, according to Quentin, could not
permit her to accept his efforts in her behalf as convincing
proof of his love for her. Maggie, echoing Louise, calls Quentin
"spoiled" (p. 116). Quentin's explanation is more theological
or philosophical:

> . . . God's power is love without limit. But when a man
> dares reach for that . . . he is only reaching for the
> power. Whoever goes to save another person with the
> lie of limitless love throws a shadow on the face of God.
> (p. 119)

A strange letter also figures in Quentin's second marriage. On
one occasion when Quentin felt disgust and pain at the thought
of his wife's past, and when she had accused him of coldness
because of it, he had written a letter to himself but had taken

no great pains to conceal it from her. In the letter, Quentin said: "The only one I will ever love is my daughter" (p. 121). His motive for writing this, he says, was "to face the worst thing I could imagine—that I could not love" (p. 121). Though love eventually dies between Maggie and Quentin, the latter feels that salvation lies in confession, in facing unflinchingly their deep hatred (p. 120). Maggie, however, prefers suicide— an act that will compel Quentin to feel like a murderer. Quentin's response, as has been said, is to choke Maggie in an effort to achieve "peace" (p. 127).

Maggie dies a short time after this incident, but "peace" eludes Quentin—at least until Holga appears on the scene representing "hope" to Quentin. Quentin is attracted to Holga for a number of reasons, not least of all because she can endure "uncertainty"; she is not looking for a "moral victory" (p. 16). These appear to be Quentin's values, too.

Louise, unlike Quentin, is not developed in a very complex manner. She was studying to be a bacteriologist when Quentin met her (pp. 69-70). Like Quentin's mother, Louise had given up her studies and her hopes for a career in order to marry. In one scene, she accuses Quentin of not wanting her to be happy: "Quentin, I saw you getting angry when I was talking about that new anti-virus vaccine" (p. 43). Quentin's reply to this charge reveals "a basic concession made by his tone of admitted bewilderment" (p. 44). Louise admits to being cold in bed, but argues that it is because Quentin is cold (p. 45). Louise is rather smug and self-righteous at times: "I don't do things," she says, "I'll be ashamed of" (p. 61). As Louise sees it, Quentin tends "to make relatives out of people" (p. 59), but if he were "mature," she claims, he would view men and women as distinct and "separate" individuals (p. 47). Louise has taken her troubles to a psychoanalyst:

I don't intend to be ashamed of myself any more, I used

to think it was normal; or even that you don't see me because I'm not worth seeing. (pp. 31-32)

It is analysis, in fact, that has helped Louise to define "maturity" in these terms: "you know another person exists . . . I'm not in analysis for nothing!" (p. 47).

Maggie is more complex than Louise. Her father deserted her mother when Maggie was eighteen months old (p. 78). Miller suggests that Maggie has spent her life searching for a "father-figure." Once, after she was grown, she had gone to upper New York to visit her father. She had had a fantasy of her father being overjoyed to see her and holding her in his arms as if she were a baby; but when she had arrived he had denied ever having known her. On the way home, Maggie, who had already met Quentin, found the latter's picture in the newspaper and went home to frame it, telling herself: "I know who I am. I'm Quentin's friend" (p. 79). In fact, the father-figure, in the person of Quentin, is translated by Maggie into "a god" (p. 79). Maggie's mother was, like the father, unsatisfactory as a parent. Maggie says that once her mother:

tried to kill me . . . with a pillow on my face, whereas . . . I would turn out bad because of her . . . like her sin. And I have her hair, and the same back. (p. 82)

When Quentin chokes Maggie, then, he is repeating what Maggie's mother did first. Note also that Miller, though he again suggests that one's fate is to a very large extent determined from birth, never implies that there is no margin of freedom or responsibility. As will be seen in the section on theme, Miller affirms freedom and responsibility.

Maggie, who never graduated from high school, is a telephone operator when Quentin first encounters her in a park (p. 74). She formerly demonstrated hair preparations, she says, but she quit that job because the men expected more than hair demonstrations from her (p. 54). Not that Maggie was a prude, for she had been quite generous with her favors. She had lived, for example, with an elderly judge for a time (no doubt a father-figure), but the judge was dead now. Maggie, who also has recourse to psychiatry, declares:

> My analyst says I used to think it was like charity—sex. Like I give to those in need? . . . Whereas I'm not an institution! (p. 89)

On their wedding day, Maggie informs Quentin:

> I was . . . with two men . . . the same day . . . I mean the same day, see. But I didn't realize it till that night. And I got very scared. (p. 97)

Louise suggests that Maggie's promiscuity is pseudo-sexuality: "You don't imagine," she tells Quentin, "a real woman goes to bed with any man who happens to come along?" (p. 62). As for Maggie, she charges her pianist with being a "fag" (p. 101) and her television director with telling "faggy jokes" (p. 102); and once, looking at Quentin's tight pants, she remarks:

> Fags wear pants like that. . . . I've known fags and some of them didn't even know themselves that they were. . . . I didn't know if you knew about that. (p. 109)

To which Quentin replies: "That's a hell of a way to reassure yourself" (p. 109).

Maggie, one might judge, has always felt "alone" (p. 78), and as a result she has no real sense of identity. For example, she likes to disguise herself in wigs (p. 84), and often she uses the name "Miss None":

> I made it up once, 'cause I can never remember a fake

name, so I just have to think of nothing and that's me!
(p. 86)

With such a background and personality chart, it is not surprising that Maggie's marriage to Quentin fails. They could not
live entirely in the "now," for the past is "holy," it has its
claims on the present. Future troubles are clearly foreshadowed
on the wedding day when Maggie shows signs of jealousy because Elsie kisses Quentin in a sexy fashion. This jealousy is
merely symptomatic of Maggie's pervasive feeling of isolation
(p. 99). Also symptomatic is the feeling of potency Maggie
experiences from spending money in an imprudent manner (p.
100). The "personal" shades into the "social" when Maggie
says: "I'm a joke that brings in money" (p. 102). It is not
strange, then, that Maggie has a record of attempted suicides
(p. 112). The girl has no religious faith to sustain her and no
strength of will with which to confront the menace of her
inner fears (p. 117). In her alcoholic fantasies, Maggie regresses
to childhood: "I want my mother," she cries (p. 117). Quentin's explanation of her behavior is that she is using him as a
screen on which to project "all the evil in the world. . . . All
the betrayal, the broken hopes, the murderous revenge" (p.
116). In the golden days of their love, Quentin could say:
"You're all love, aren't you?"—and Maggie could reply: "That's
all I am!" (p. 87); at the end of the marriage, however, Quentin says: "Do the hardest thing of all—see your own hatred,
and live!" (p. 120). Maggie will not accept the hostility and
aggression that are in her; she insists on the fiction of her "innocence":

You gonna be good now? 'Cause all I am . . . is love.
And sex. (p. 124)

Such "innocence" is not of this world, and a few months after
this statement Maggie destroys herself.

Holga, like Louise, is sketched in rather lightly. Unlike Louise or Quentin's mother, Holga refuses to quit her job as an archaeologist in order to marry (p. 14). Unlike Maggie, who also continued working after marriage, Holga can face the truth about life: "one doesn't want to lose the past, even if it's dreadful" (p. 13). Like Maggie, Holga had once tried to kill herself, but failing in that attempt, she learned to "kiss" her "broken life" (p. 24). During the war in Europe, Holga "became a courier for the officers who were planning to assassinate Hitler" (p. 16). Later Holga was detained in a concentration camp (p. 13). Unlike Quentin's first two wives, Holga is "not a woman who must be reassured every minute" (p. 14); she is not supremely confident of her own "good faith" (p. 15); and she shares Quentin's guilt for the sins of mankind (p. 23).

All the characters are part of a complex thematic pattern, and they will be discussed again in the final section. A few remarks on Quentin's character *as* character, however, would seem to be in order here.

Quentin, as I have tried to suggest, is one of Miller's most interesting creations. Whether he is more "real" or complex than, say, Willy Loman or Eddie Carbone, is an open question. At any rate, Miller deserves credit for seeking to depict a figure fully rounded in terms of modern knowledge. He has obviously not been content to project still another dramatized case history—whether he has *in fact* avoided doing so is another question; nor has he retreated into the often too pessimistic theater of the Absurdist school. Characteristically, Miller has tried to present the "whole truth"—but once again, whether he has even approached doing so in actuality is another matter. Aim in *After the Fall* would seem to have outdistanced achievement.

Some readers may feel that Quentin, in spite of his self-torment, does not really come to grips with his problems in an entirely satisfactory manner. In a sense, Miller whitewashes Quentin in his relations with his mother because the focus is almost wholly on *her* guilt and on Quentin's "complicity"; this

complicity, however, is rather passive, and not necessarily blameworthy in all respects. Who would seriously censure Quentin
for refusing to place his future in the hands of an obviously
incompetent businessman like his father? True, economic
factors are partly the cause of the father's losses; yet the man
is shown as overly dependent on his wife and far from intelligent or capable. Who would insist that Quentin ought to have
surrendered his hopes for the future and a career of his own?
The play reveals that people who do this—such as Quentin's
mother and Louise—tend to regret it later and as a consequence
make others unhappy. Who would share Quentin's vehement
denunciation of his mother because she left him to go to
Atlantic City with her husband? Why such murderous rage
in Quentin—boy *and* man—over this seemingly trivial incident?
Quentin betrays signs of an Oedipus complex, yet Miller resists,
as I have said, interpreting the experience of his protagonist in
such a light. Granted, the hatred for the mother is owned; the
fact that Quentin has been spoiled is there; the contempt for
the father is admitted ("[Dan] was always the one who idolized
the old man, and I saw through him from the beginning," [p. 8]);
and quite evident is Quentin's inability to achieve lasting happiness with any woman; but the strong love for the mother that
would normally accompany these facts is absent. The reader
may not share Quentin's powerful conviction about his mother's
"crime," that her guilt is attributable to a crime equal in kind
to the Nazi's murder of the Jews, nor feel that Quentin's attachment to his mother has been adequately encompassed by the
rather embarrassing remark: "I love that nut. . . ." One may feel
that Quentin indulges in too much rationalization, that too
much of his experience is translated too quickly into intellectual
formulations without sufficient inspection of the affective content of that experience. Miller is certainly to be commended for
withstanding the oversimplification that mothers are the root
cause of evil in the universe. Yet it is difficult to escape the feeling, in view of the fact that so much is made of Quentin's and

Maggie's past, that there is any other cause of evil as crucial as the parental in *their lives*.

The worst thing that Quentin can accuse himself of, he feels, is failure to love. We might all confess to as much, and yet fail to be more specific about other, perhaps smaller and less fashionable, shortcomings which are, *for us*, much more to the point. Favoring Quentin, Miller often stacks the cards against the other characters. Louise is an example. When after an altercation with Quentin about the meaning of "maturity," an altercation in which sensible things are said on both sides, Louise is made to say: "I'm not in analysis for nothing!" the reader suspects that the game is rigged. It is laudable that Miller wants to see all around his subject and characters, for he seeks to universalize Quentin's experience—he is not merely trying to shift the burden of guilt onto others. Not *merely*; yet the impression remains that there *is* this shifting of guilt in a self-justifying manner on Quentin's part, and that the shifting continues until the end of the play. True, there are two sides to every story; but in art, and here we return to the limitations of point of view in *Fall*, those sides are best portrayed *objectively*, and not in one side's monologue or memory of the affair. In the confessional box, the penitent confesses *his* sins alone; on the analyst's couch, the analysand comes to grips with *his* neurosis. Certainly, Quentin's choking of Maggie is a serious affair, but often enough, Quentin is as infantile in his reactions as is Maggie. Quentin's propensity for writing notes for his wives to discover is pertinent here. How many men keep a log in which to record the amount of time they devote to their wives? It seems clear that Quentin is deceiving himself about the guilt he felt over Louise's dislike for her own reflection. It is more likely that Quentin is projecting the dislike *he* felt for his wife's fading looks. Miller seems deluded, too; he says that his hero feels guilt "even for what he did not do" (*Life*, February 7, 1964). This is neurotic. Furthermore, Quentin lacks the compensating grace of humor. He is not depicted with the

requisite detachment. The stilted, stereotyped language of Willy
Loman was fitting in *Salesman* because it was one with Willy's
character and with the texture and theme of the play. The frequently stilted and self-conscious utterances of Quentin are
disturbing because *Fall* is not about the death of a salesman, but
about the Rebirth of Man. Quentin, in other words, is an inadequate vehicle to carry the message of modern humanistic
values. Consequently, language is here, for the first time in a
Miller play I believe, a major defect. Again it is largely a question
of technique.

Technique: and not, it must be stressed, the theme of the
play—which caused so much concern when *Fall* was first presented. Miller, in response to accusations that he was shame-
fully autobiographical in *After the Fall*, has rightly argued that
such questions are irrelevant and that the critic must properly
"grapple with the objective meaning of the work at hand." According to Miller, the "value" of a specific play "depends, or
ought to, on its general application to other men besides" the
author (*Life*). What, then, is the theme of Miller's play?

In the final two and a half pages of *After the Fall*, Quentin
sums up the intent of the play: "Look, I'll say it. It's really all
I came to say" (p. 126). And what Quentin says amounts to
this: Man must learn to love, not in ignorance of his defects
and death wishes, but in spite of them; man must face life with
self-knowledge and self-forgiveness.

The first thing to remark about Miller's theme—*as* theme,
that is—is that, the disparaging attitude of some Broadway reviewers to it notwithstanding, the same idea has been expressed
by some of the most important minds of the past two centuries.
The idea is present, for example, in Dostoevsky's *Karamazov*
(and one should recall here that Miller—see *Harper's*, August
1958—has credited Ibsen and Dostoevsky with teaching him
what a writer "was supposed to be"):

There is only one means of salvation [says Father Zos-

sima] . . . take yourself and make yourself responsible
for all men's sins . . . that is the truth, you know, friends,
for as soon as you sincerely make yourself responsible for
everything and for all men, you will see at once that it is
really so, and that you are to blame for every one and
for all things . . . no one can judge a criminal, until he
recognizes that he is just such a criminal as the man
standing before him, and that he perhaps is more than
all men to blame for that crime.

The same idea can be found expressed in the work of Albert
Schweitzer and Carl Jung. One might go even further in defense
of the nobility of Miller's theme as such and note that the idea
is implicit in the Talmudic saying: "Him who destroys one
human life, the Scripture regards as if he had destroyed the
whole world." It is also implicit in Christ's equation of desire
and act in regard to lust—and if the equation be accepted as
valid for lust, why not for death wishes, providing those wishes
are not consciously rejected? Quentin goes further, of course,
and actually chokes Maggie. It may or may not be in order to
charge Miller with failing to distinguish legal and perhaps moral
guilt from "mystical" and psychological guilt. How explicit need
a playwright be? The crucial question, it seems to me, lies elsewhere. If the theme is such as Quentin summarizes it, the
reader has a right—since this is a play and not a sermon or
lecture—to see that theme embodied in action, to see the play
build concretely and convincingly to its concluding insight. In
short, rationalization should follow dramatization.

Quentin's mother failed in love because she turned from her
husband to her son for emotional support. She showed that she
could be inconstant with her son, too, as the Atlantic City
incident demonstrates. Modern psychological theory tends, with
Quentin, to regard suicide as murder of an introjected "other";
hence, many of the characters in Fall are "murderers." Quentin's attempted suicide as a child was an expression of murder-

ous rage against his parent. Maggie's suicide is also relevant to
the theme. Louise, by refusing to accept her share of guilt, must
be regarded as destructive through lack of self-knowledge ("one
must know oneself," says Miller in the *Post*, "but no man knows
himself who cannot face the murder in him, the sly and ever-
lasting complicity with the forces of destruction"). Quentin's
father is made "guilty" because he voted in an election too soon,
as Quentin sees it, after his wife's death. Moving out beyond
the family, Quentin points the accusing finger at society. Lou
has betrayed Quentin and others with his lies about Russia.
Mickey is prepared to betray Lou. Quentin "betrays" Lou because he feels a sense of "joy" in his release from the burden of
protecting his friend. Lou's suicide would seem to be still
another "murder." Elsie is ready to betray her husband with
Quentin. Hence, Quentin, Mickey, and Elsie all appear to be
guilty for Lou's death. Felice's divorce is still another failure in
love. Not content with the local scene, Quentin moves toward
an even wider universalization of the theme. Holga is brought
forward, in part, to link Quentin's family, his marriages, and his
friends' fate with the Nazi horror, which was perhaps the most
total manifestation of man's inhumanity in history. The "burning cities of Europe" and "the death of love" taught Holga and
Quentin the same truth—"we are very dangerous!" (p. 128).

There is something a little too pat about this theme. For all
its non-representational machinery, *After the Fall* remains very
much an old-fashioned thesis play. It is almost too heavily didactic. The attempt to encompass such a vast range of data almost
automatically precludes working in depth in any one segment.
Economic influences are introduced in the 1929 crash which
rends Quentin's family, in Maggie's inability to buy self-respect,
and in Quentin's failure to be happy as a "successful" lawyer.
Political motivation appears in the sequence involving Lou and
Mickey. Most of the economic and political significance of the
play, however, disappears after Act One. The latter half of
the play concentrates on what Miller would probably call "the

nature of the human being himself" but which really comes down to psychological, or character, study. As a result, the economic and political dimensions of *Fall* seem rather thin and not really worked into the texture or substance of the play. Quentin and Maggie are solidly drawn characters, but the other figures are, on the whole, little more than puppets. With its diversity of characters and experiences, *Fall* ought to possess some of the analogical richness of Elizabethan tragedy (I am using "analogy" here in the sense as developed chiefly by the Scholastic and Neo-Scholastic philosophers and as applied to the drama by Francis Fergusson in *The Idea of a Theater*); due to its over-conceptualized approach, however, what is actually projected is a kind of thematic "monism"—a flat, impoverished, only partly convincing picture of life which leaves one with the feeling that significant differences in characters and experiences have not been acknowledged. Needless to say, it is precisely the "differences" that convey the sense of life to us in the drama. *After the Fall* is simply too much of the same.

The extension of guilt from the personal to the social, the latter in this case symbolized by the Nazi concentration camp, may be a perfectly valid generalization. In dramatic terms, though, that generalization is not made convincing. There is too much of an air of contrivance. By employing a loose and open form, Miller, in his haste to articulate an intellectual formulation that will tidily sum up our present plight, is tempted to circumvent, or to leapfrog over, that need for close inspection of matter, that necessity to definitely particularize time and place and gradually accumulate significant details, which results in a tight mesh of probability. To put it another way, unity in *Fall* is chiefly mechanical, merely verbal. At one point, Quentin says: "some unseen web of connection between people is simply not there" (p. 44), and near the end, echoing Louise, he remarks: "We are all separate people" (p. 119). If you accept these lines at face value, you might argue that the form is appropriate to the theme. It would not be prudent, however, to place too much stress on these lines because they are expressions of a particular mood—the first arising during a quarrel with Louise, the second in the final scene with Maggie; moreover, the lines are at odds with the main thematic thrust of the play. It can be more cogently argued, perhaps, that the form is inappropriate to the theme because what else does *Fall* assert if not that all men are *one*—one in hatred, one in evil, one in guilt, but also one in their need for love and hope and courage and understanding? The form generously allows for focusing on moments scattered in time and place; it does not accommodate, it is not hospitable to, that sense of relatedness that it is the burden of Quentin to propound for three hours in the theater. Holga is a good example. As a concrete link with the "burning cities of Europe," Holga is not entirely adequate. It is possible, of course, that Holga could be part of an abortive anti-Hitler coup—but is it probable? More to the point, does Miller make it *seem* probable? Why was Holga sent to a concentration camp? She was not betrayed, she says; she was not a Jew; and she was not a communist (p. 13). There is only a suggestion that before the war was ended she had rebelled in some way against the regime (p. 16). But in *what* way? Furthermore, Holga is unsatisfactory merely as a woman in love. She has not a single fault. She is seen too much, in spite of Quentin's passion to discern things clearly, with the blurred vision of early romantic emotion. Holga, finally, is too much the foil to the other women in Quentin's life. She remains merely another "instance" to "prove the theme."

This same scarcity of details, this continuing attempt to reduce a multitude of differences to a single formula, is unfortunately everywhere in evidence in *Fall*. The extension of guilt is, in the main, merely asserted—it is not made to seem "real." As a result, the theme, which is broad but not very deep, is vitiated and its relevance blurred.

A Note on *The Misfits*

It was not surprising that, during his absence from the
theater, Miller should write a film play. The present study has
more than once indicated Miller's use of cinematic devices in
his plays. In the published version of *The Misfits*, Miller says:

> Movies . . . have . . . created a particular way of seeing
> life, and their swift transitions, their sudden bringing
> together of disparate images, their effect of documenta-
> tion inevitable in photography, their economy of story-
> telling, and their concentration on mute action have in-
> filtrated the novel and play writing—especially the latter
> —without being confessed to or, at times, being con-
> sciously realized at all. (pp. ix-x)

The Misfits deals with a group of men in the modern West who
hunt horses, not for the romance and adventure that they once
found in the work when the horses would be sold as Christmas
presents to children, for the latter in our mechanized age have
scooters now, but for money alone, fully aware that the horses
will be slaughtered for canned dog food. For Biff Loman, the
West had seemed the answer to his frustration and discontent
with city life. Miller suggests that Biff, in the world of *The
Misfits*, would be similarly unhappy in the wide open spaces. As
one of the "misfits," Gay, puts it:

> God damn them all! They changed it. Changed it all
> around. They smeared it all over with blood, turned it
> into shit and money just like everything else. (p. 129)

Clearly, then, there is continuity of theme between Miller's
plays and his film work. Other examples might also be cited.
Perhaps the most interesting point to be made is the relationship between Maggie in *After the Fall* and the "golden girl" (p.

7), Roslyn, in *The Misfits*. The biographical aspect of these two characters is not at issue here. The problem is an aesthetic one, for Miller has lifted Roslyn bodily from the film, changed her name and address, and presented us with Maggie in *After the Fall*. The remarks that follow in regard to Roslyn should call to mind what has been said earlier in this chapter about Maggie.

Although Roslyn's parents were not "there" when she was a child, Roslyn, in her loneliness, often finds herself wishing that her mother were near to comfort her (pp. 15-16). Roslyn has never finished high school (p. 17). Guido describes her as "dumb" (p. 21). Roslyn is embarrassed, and likewise her lover Gay, by her past (p. 46). As Guido sees it, however, Roslyn has the "gift of life"—she really wants to "live" (p. 48). Roslyn even talks like Maggie: "Birds must be brave. . . . Whereas they're so small, you know?" (p. 37). The film ends with Roslyn and Gay leaving the past behind and driving off hopefully into a starry night, both of them vowing to follow *their* star and to teach their child not to be afraid.

The Misfits has been called a soap opera, especially in its insistence upon the "love" cliché of the Fifties. The soap opera aspect is certainly evident; but one need not concur that "love" is *always* thematic hokum. "Love" is open to many definitions. At issue is *After the Fall*, for here Miller is clearly aiming at a "love" that is more substantial than mere romantic ecstasy. True, Quentin's relationship to Holga is marred by a failure to see the woman as a whole person; yet the play is striving, in its general though awkward design, toward a responsible and adult viewpoint. In this respect, then, it is superior to *The Misfits*.

CHAPTER SEVEN

Incident at Vichy

Incident at Vichy (1964), written a few months after the New York production of *After the Fall*, is a long one-act play. As the title suggests, the action takes place in France during the Second World War. A group of characters have been arrested by the Nazis on the charge that they are Jews, and the dramatic question focuses on the various reactions of the captives to the enormous evil that confronts them.

There is a single set: "A place of detention":

> At the right a corridor leads to a turning and an un-
> seen door to the street. Across the back is a structure
> with two grimy window panes in it—perhaps an office, in
> any case a private room with a door opening from it at
> the left.
> A long bench stands in front of this room, facing a
> large empty area whose former use is unclear but which
> suggests a warehouse, perhaps, an armory, or part of a
> railroad station not used by the public. Two small boxes
> stand apart on either side of the bench. (p. 1)

There is also unity of time and action; that is, there is a single movement of the plot that corresponds precisely with the actual time of representation in the theater, which, according to the viewers, is about ninety-five minutes.

Miller carefully sets the stage for his action:

> When light begins to rise, six men and a boy of fifteen
> are discovered on the bench in attitudes expressive of
> their personalities and functions, frozen there like mem-
> bers of a small orchestra at the moment before they
> begin to play.
>
> As normal light comes on, their positions flow out of
> the frieze. It appears that they do not know one another
> and are sitting like people thrown together in a public
> place, mutually curious but self-occupied. However, they
> are anxious and frightened and tend to make themselves
> small and unobtrusive. (p. 1)

Exposition reveals that the characters on the bench have been
arrested, but the reason for their arrest is not directly stated at
once. The extreme nervousness of the men, however, establishes the fact that their charge is a serious one. An air of
mysterious evil hangs over the bench. An electrician, Bayard,
says: "You begin wishing you'd committed a crime, you know?
Something definite" (p. 3). Thus, the point of attack occurs
within the first two pages of dialogue; the characters have
reached a turning point in their lives, and something vital is at
stake; the major dramatic question, moreover, is also suggested
in the varying reactions of the men to the problem that is
before them.

Marchand, a businessman, is the one captive who acts self-
confident: "It's perfectly obvious they're making a routine identity check" (p. 4). Lebeau, a painter, is not so sure about that—
he suspects "some racial . . . implication" (p. 4). As the men
discuss their personal plight, the dialogue frequently carries
them into abstractions and the larger issues involved. Bayard, a
Marxist, blames the "monopolies" for the evil of the war: "Big
business is out to make slaves of everyone, that's why you're
here" (p. 6). Lebeau, who admits that he is not a philosopher,
tends to disparage reason: "don't ask what it means; you're not
God, you can't tell what anything means" (p. 6).

Tension is augmented by the repeated appearances of a police guard who strolls up and down the corridor with a revolver in view, silently eyeing the captives.

Monceau, an actor, agrees with the businessman: "I think as soon as they start, it shouldn't take long"—to which Lebeau replies: "Did they measure your nose?" (p. 7). The "racial implications" of the arrest now become clear.

> The office door opens and the Major comes out. He is twenty-eight, a wan but well-built man; there is something ill about him. He walks with a slight limp, passing the line of men as he goes toward the corridor. (p. 10)

The appearance of the Major not only heightens the tension but also, through exposition, establishes motivation for a later crisis. A waiter appears and says:

> I serve him breakfast every morning. Tell you the truth, he's really not a bad fellow. Regular army, see, not one of these S. S. bums. Got wounded somewhere, so they stuck him back here. (p. 11)

With the situation established, then, Miller introduces the two chief actors in his drama. Leduc, a psychoanalyst, and Von Berg, an Austrian prince, are brought in, along with an Old Jew, by the police. A hint of Leduc's character is immediately conveyed when a detective warns him: "Don't you give me any more trouble now" (p. 12).

The procedure is for the police to call the captives, one by one, into the office. This is another device calculated to produce tension. Marchand is the first of the men to enter the office. During his absence the other men continue to discuss their dangerous situation. Bayard, who works in the railroad yards, reports that a trainload of Jews were taken away the other day

(p. 16). Monceau, however, persists in being optimistic: "A lot of people have been volunteering for work in Germany" (p. 16); besides, he adds, the "Germans are still *people*" (p. 19, italics in original). For Bayard the Germans are Fascists, and that fact settles the matter. For Leduc they are simply human beings—and what could be worse? (p. 20). Von Berg, upon learning that Leduc had studied in Vienna, asks the latter if he had known Von Berg's cousin, Baron Kessler; but Leduc, "with an odd coolness," denies having known the man. According to Von Berg, Kessler was "extremely democratic" (p. 20). This exchange is important foreshadowing for the climax of the play. Von Berg's position on the bench puzzles the other men, for he is an aristocrat, a Catholic, and apolitical, and, consequently, they do not know why he was arrested. Perhaps, they imply, the Nazis made a mistake. Von Berg affirms his pride in his name and family, as represented by his title, and declares that he would not dishonor himself (p. 22). This is also preparation for the climax of the play.

The office door opens then and Marchand exits—with a pass to freedom. Says Lebeau: "I could have sworn he was a Jew!" (p. 25). Bayard, Monceau, and Leduc continue to indulge in a philosophical analysis of the situation: Bayard believes that one must draw strength from identifying the self with the working classes; Monceau's strength lies in his ability to fashion his "own reality in this world" (p. 29); and Leduc amuses himself by being cynical about both positions. Von Berg agrees with Leduc; one cannot pin one's hopes upon a specific class—only a relatively small number of "people of integrity" spell the difference between civilization and descent into utter barbarism (pp. 33-34). Once again, this is important foreshadowing for the crisis and climax of the play.

The waiter, who has spoken to someone that knows the truth, reports the words that end any doubts the prisoners may have had about the danger of their position: "People get burned up in furnaces. It's not to work. They burn you up in Poland" (p. 35). This is precisely the half-way mark of the play. At this point, Bayard is removed to the office—never to return.

Desperate now, Leduc suggests that they try to escape. Von Berg, who lacks "strength in his hands," asks to be left out of consideration (p. 37); Monceau, who still will not believe that the Germans could do such a vile thing, also refuses to act (p. 38); the other prisoners say nothing and do nothing. Leduc is shocked by their passivity.

Suddenly the Major reappears, this time with the Professor from the German Race Institute. The Major asks for permission to be released from his duties, but the Professor is inflexible. The latter's threat to report the Major is sufficient to quell the soldier. Says the Professor: "The Army's responsibility is quite as great as mine here" (p. 43).

Lebeau finally agrees to try to escape, warning Leduc, however, that he is as "weak as a chicken" (p. 44). The boy is also willing to make a run for freedom. Now it is Leduc who is reluctant to try the escape because Lebeau and the boy are not very strong: "I wanted to get away," he says, "not just slaughtered" (p. 48). When the boy makes a dash for the door, however, Leduc casts caution aside and follows him. But the Major, who has been drinking, appears and blocks their path. This is the turning point of the play, for Leduc's inability to escape here forces the resolution. At first, the Major appeals to their sympathy: "this is all as inconceivable to me as it is to you" (p. 53); but Leduc will have none of this, for he says, "I'd believe you if you shot yourself. And better yet, if you took a few of them with you" (p. 53). Stung, and feeling guilty, the Major shouts: "You—goddamned Jews!" (p. 54). In his defense, the Major argues that no one can be responsible in the modern world because every man is a prisoner of another (p. 55). The incident ends with still another lamb—this time Lebeau—led into the office. Monceau and the boy quickly follow him, and the Old Jew, Von Berg, and Leduc are remaining.

Leduc asks Von Berg, who will be released because he is not a Jew, to inform his wife about his fate. Von Berg feels a sense of guilt: "it will not be easy for me to walk out of here" (p. 60). As they talk, the Old Jew is taken into the office. Leduc grows increasingly bitter, denouncing the fact that he had been stupid enough to live his life by ideals. Von Berg protests, for he cannot accept a world without ideals:

> There are ideals. . . . There are people who would find it easier to die than stain one finger with this murder. They exist. . . . People for whom everything is *not* permitted, foolish people and ineffectual, but they do exist and will not dishonor their traditon. (pp. 65-66)

Leduc's reply is that every gentile harbors, if only unconsciously, a "dislike if not a hatred for the Jews" (pp. 66-67). Von Berg denies this. Leduc, "with a wild pity in his voice," explains that the Jew is only a scapegoat for the gentile: "Each man has his Jew; it is the other" (p. 66). The dramatic question of the play—"How should these men confront the evil of Nazism?"—is now sharply focused at the resolution of the drama. Leduc leads Von Berg to the challenge of the theme:

> now . . . you must see that you have [your Jew]—the man whose death leaves you relieved that you are not him. . . . And that is why there is nothing and will be nothing—until you face your own complicity with this . . . your own humanity. (p. 66)

In the face of Von Berg's denials, Leduc informs the Prince that Baron Kessler, far from being a democrat, was a vicious Nazi who "helped to remove all the Jewish doctors from the medical school" in Vienna (p. 67). Von Berg, "stunned, inward-seeing," admits that he had heard of it, but that he "had forgotten it" (p. 67). The crisis is prepared when Leduc says:

> It's not your guilt I want, it's your responsibility . . . if
> you had understood that Baron Kessler was . . . in some
> small and frightful part—doing your will. You might have
> done something then. . . . (pp. 68-69)

As Von Berg is removed to the office, he asks: "What can ever
save us?"

When Von Berg returns from the office, he has his pass to
freedom. He does not hesitate. Quickly he hands the pass
to Leduc:

> *Leduc backs away, his hands springing to cover his eyes in*
> *the awareness of his own guilt.*
> Leduc—*a plea in his voice:* I wasn't asking you to do
> this! (p. 69)

Nevertheless, Leduc—"his eyes wide in awe and terror"—dashes
outside to freedom. This is the climax of the play; and the conclusion follows immediately. The play ends with a new group of
prisoners being herded into the detention room, and with Von
Berg and the Major "forever incomprehensible to one another,
looking into each other's eyes" (p. 70).

In his review of *Incident at Vichy*, Henry Hewes calls the play
an "illustrated essay," a "dramatic essay," and ends by declaring:
"Instead of incident we get instances." Robert Brustein takes a
similar line: "since the action is mainly restricted to a bench, it
cannot help being static for long periods and melodramatic for
short one." Douglas Watt calls the escape plans "bits of contrived theatrics." Thus, Miller is accused, on the one hand, of
presenting an excessively abstract and didactic play, and, on the
other, of seeking to enliven the static scene by indulging in mere
melodramatic decoration. Is this fair?

The description and analysis given above should suggest an
answer. *Incident at Vichy* is a play, not a sermon. True, there is
a good deal of "talk" in the play. Aside from the fact that Shaw
and Sartre have demonstrated that "talk" can be dramatic, the

point must be stressed that Miller's play has a definite dramatic
structure. There is, as has been said, complete unity of time,
place, and action. (There is also unity of theme.) The point of
attack comes almost at once. The major dramatic question is
immediately focused, and the question continues to motivate
every word and movement in the play until its resolution. One
should be able to detect, in looking over the description and
analysis, not only small patterns of crisis, climax, and conclusion,
but an overall line of steadily rising tension. The objection that
confining action to a bench causes the play to be static is not
only contrary to the particular fact of this play, but in a general
sense, seems absurd as well. As Howard Taubman rightly says:
"The very fact of the steady attrition of victims is in itself a
dramatic device of unfaltering suspense." The attempted escape
from the detention room, far from being mere "theatrics,"
strikes me as wholly credible; in any group of actual prisoners,
one or two of them at least would risk a dash for freedom; and,
moreover, in the play itself, Miller makes the attempt convincing through the argumentation that the plan arouses, a discussion that reveals various human reactions to such a problem,
and, especially, by making the instigator, Leduc, an angry and
desperate man, precisely the kind of a character who would
make such a move. Miller's control of his medium is evident
from his careful foreshadowing of events; Von Berg's climactic
behavior, for example, is prepared for step-by-step, yet that
preparation is never crude or transparent.

The technical advance of *Incident at Vichy* over *After the
Fall*—or, to express it another way, Miller's return to the
technical mastery of *Death of a Salesman*, *The Crucible*, and
A View from the Bridge—needs no extended underlining.
Incident at Vichy is one of Miller's most finished works.

A close analysis of the characters in the play will demon-
strate further that the judgment is a valid one. Von Berg, as
has been stated, is an Austrian prince; he is also a Roman
Catholic and politically ignorant, which is presumably a class

defect because the Prince explains that most nobles "never took responsibility" for the Nazis (p. 22). For Von Berg the Nazis are to be censured on aesthetic grounds—they are simply "vulgar" (p. 23). He asks: "Can people with respect for art go about hounding Jews?" (p. 24). For all his weakness, however, there is a vein of iron and good sense in this aristocrat. The iron stems from his pride in his tradition; the good sense is evident in his belief in "certain aristocrats. . . . And in certain common people"— in short, in real individuals, not in Nazi and Marxist abstractions (p. 33). Physically, Von Berg is weak (p. 37), but the will, as the play's climax shows, is not dependent on muscle. That Von Berg's response to events is not wholly aesthetic in the beginning is apparent from his reaction to the Nazi's murdering of his musicians in Vienna. He had wanted to destroy himself then, he says, because so many of his friends were indifferent to the killings (p. 61). That Von Berg could contemplate suicide reveals his conviction that a life without ideals is not worth living (p. 61), and this conviction helps to make his final action credible. It is, in fact, a certain innocence about the man—"I know so little about people" (p. 63), "I have no great . . . facility with women" (p. 60)—that also helps to make his self-sacrifice understandable. Perhaps a more calculating man, even a more intelligent man, would have convinced himself that in the circumstances of Vichy, self-sacrifice was not the way. Moreover, given a man of the limited reasoning powers of Von Berg—he is, in some respects, as he himself puts it, "foolish . . . and ineffectual" (p. 65)—it is made convincing that he might hoodwink himself about Baron Kessler (p. 67). Even his Catholicism is made to function in an active manner. At the resolution of the play he cries: "What can *save* us? (p. 68, italics mine); this would seem to be the way in which a Christian would look at the problem—and his act of self-sacrifice, of course, takes Christ for its model. Von Berg, it will be seen then, is a sufficiently complex and believable dramatic creation.

Leduc is in many ways Von Berg's opposite, or foil. As a psychoanalyst, Leduc has been trained to be introspective and analytical. He is also, unlike Von Berg, a calculating man (p. 14). His professional role enables him to arrive at the same conclusions, however, that Von Berg holds in regard to the opium of Marxist propaganda—he sees, that is, not labels but people (p. 20). Yet even Leduc can harbor built-in prejudices, such as, his belief that an "aristocracy is . . . always behind a reactionary regime" (p. 22). Leduc has an icy sense of fact; to Monceau's argument that one must create oneself, the doctor asks: "But when they tell you to open your fly" (that is, to see if you are a circumcised Jew)? (p. 49). Leduc is an "activist" —he is unable to appreciate "passivity" (p. 49); he is afraid that "Jew and gentile both" have been "trained to die" (p. 51). That Leduc is no plaster saint is, to take but one example for the present, evident from his talk about his wife. At first he asks Von Berg to inform his wife that he was sent to the furnaces (p. 59); later, however, he confesses that he is no longer in love with his wife and that he had wanted revenge on her because he would never have been captured had he not gone out to get medicine for her. "God, at a time like this," he exclaims, "to think of taking vengeance on her! What scum we are!" (p. 63).

The other characters are less complex than Von Berg and Leduc, but all of them are dramatically striking. Lebeau, the painter, is "a bearded, unkempt man of twenty-five" (p. 2). He admits to being "utterly confused" by the evil that faces him (p. 6). He assumes the stance that, in effect, art "must not mean, but be" (p. 7). Feeling himself an outcast from middle class society, Lebeau implies that all business is organized stealing (p. 9): "Whenever a people starts to work hard, watch out, they're going to kill somebody" (p. 10). His own wish is to "work without making work a god!" (p. 10). Miller suggests, however, that Lebeau is a contemptible weakling. He blames his mother, for example, for his present plight:

In 1939 we were packed for America. Suddenly my
mother wouldn't leave the furniture. I'm here because of
a brass bed and some fourth-rate crockery. And a stub-
born, ignorant woman. (p. 6)

Lebeau's philosophy is that every man must think of himself:
"What the hell am I supposed to think of? Who're you thinking of?" (p. 28). He reveals that a Jew—he means himself—
grows to "believe" what the Nazis say about him. Reality,
Lebeau confesses, is simply too much for him: "I could never
paint what I saw, only what I imagined" (p. 51); "you get
tired of believing in the truth . . . tired of seeing things clearly"
(p. 50).

Reality is also too gross for the actor, Monceau: "One must
create one's own reality . . . I'm an actor, we do this all the
time" (p. 29). As Monceau sees it, life is merely a problem of
mind over matter, or the power of positive thinking: "everyone
said I was crazy to stay in the [acting] profession. But I did,
and I imposed my idea on others" (p. 49). Failing to distinguish between unequal situations, neglecting the difference between the theater and the place of detention, Monceau, it is
not surprising, is similarly deluded in respect to the nature of
Nazism: "the Germans are not illogical; there's no conceivable
advantage for them in furnaces" (p. 37). Monceau is not only
ignorant of the "illogical" evil that pervades the racism of the
Germans, he is further mistaken about the status of law in a
world in which certain assumptions about man's nature are no
longer taken for granted. (As Lebeau, in one of his more lucid
moments, expresses it: "After the Romans and the Greeks and
the Renaissance . . . you know what this means?") "I go on
the assumption," reports Monceau, "that if I obey the law
with dignity I will live in peace" (p. 52). Although one might
doubt the validity of Monceau's insight into reality, the actor
insists that one must, finally, conform to the world as it is,
for, he argues, if the majority did not want a specific law they

would simply abolish it. Standing squarely on a philosophy without visible means of support, Monceau demands that Leduc cease his "romantic challenges!" (p. 52). After this indulgence in semantic sleight-of-hand, Monceau disappears into the police office. He is not heard from again.

Bayard is described as a young man, "poorly but cleanly dressed, with a certain muscular austerity in his manner" (p. 2). This description fits the role that Bayard performs in the world—he is an electrician in the freight yards. In spite of his Marxist jargon ("Big business is out to make slaves of everyone" [p. 6]. . . . "The bourgeoisie sold France" [p. 30] . . . "the future is Socialist" [p. 31], etc.), Bayard is very much the Rousseauistic "romantic." He refuses to agree with Leduc that human nature has a propensity to evil as well as to good. No, argues Bayard, the Germans are bad because they are Fascists —if they became, Bayard implies, Marxists they would then be admirable fellows (p. 20). The truth, which has an unpleasant tendency to contradict theories, does not seem to be especially important; like Monceau, Bayard urges positive thinking: "You'd better ram a viewpoint up your spine or you'll break in half" (p. 31)—the need, then, is for a "*a* viewpoint," not necessarily one that corresponds with the measurements of the situation. Bayard has no regard for the individual—only the mass is relevant: "You can't make sense of this on a personal basis" (p. 31); thus, he accepts alienation: "How can my spirit [in such a world as this] be where my body is?"—and his spirit, he roundly affirms, is in the future (p. 32). The most vital part of Bayard, then, is unrelated to the existential area of his operations; he is waiting for the great day "when the working class is master of the world" (p. 32). Is this "mystical"? Not according to Bayard: "A human being," he says, "has to glory in the facts" (p. 33).

The Major also stresses the "facts," at least as he sees them. And, for him, the facts are that the old world of Judaic-Christian and humanistic values is irretrievably gone:

There are no persons any more, don't you see that?
There will never be persons again. What do I care if
you love me? . . . What am I, a dog that I must be
loved? (p. 54)

According to the Major, man has no responsibility for evil, and
to ask for man's responsibility is to ask for his self-destruction:

I have you [to Leduc] at the end of this revolver—
indicates the Professor—he has me—and somebody has
somebody else. Now tell me. (p. 55)

It is part of Von Berg's office to refute the Major.

Several reviewers of *Incident at Vichy* suggested that Miller's
characters were flat, mere didactic symbols. When I discuss the
theme of the play, I shall argue that *Incident*, like *Crucible*, is
a philosophical melodrama, and in this respect Miller is working in the tradition of Shaw and Sartre. One might also reply
to the criticism of the reviewers by pointing out that Miller's
play meets several crucial tests in respect to dramatic characterization. For one thing, the description of Von Berg and
Leduc discusssed above reveals that both characters have several
traits, a fact that should suggest that they are more than mere
"public symbols." For another thing, Von Berg, Leduc, and
the Major grow in the course of the play: Von Berg moves
from a stance of detached sympathy but essential irresponsibil-
ity for the Nazi evil, through a revelation that he had deceived
himself about his complicity, to a position of responsibility,
even unto death, for the evil represented by the place of detention; Leduc moves from a self-righteous conviction of his moral
superiority to Nazi and to passive victim alike, through cynicism
and loss of ideals, to a final shattering of his lofty pose of
superiority and to a rebirth of his belief in the human po-
tentiality for good; the Major moves from a distinctly human
concern that he be well-thought of through his claim that the

evil is inconceivable to him, through growing guilt feelings and resultant rage against his accusers, to a stance in which he denies freedom of the will and, in the process of renouncing this human faculty, cuts himself off "forever" from comprehending the purposes of a man like Von Berg. Finally, the unity of opposites between Von Berg and Leduc grows increasingly binding. If Von Berg walks out the door to freedom, he remains, in the eyes of Leduc, a coward and a hypocrite, a proof that idealism is a fatal illusion. If Von Berg forfeits his pass through acceptance of his complicity in evil, he vindicates the latent goodness in the human animal—but at the cost of his life. Between these two poles lies tension and conflict, and a guarantee that the characters involved must grow and, in the act of growing, reveal the theme of Miller's play.

And it is the theme of the play that has occasioned critical dispute. *Incident at Vichy*, says Howard Taubman, "returns the theater to greatness." Henry Hewes, who finds fault with the play, yet feels that it has "provocative substance and a certain beauty. . . ." But Robert Brustein can find nothing good in the play; he disagrees with his fellow reviewers: "It has about as much vigor and beauty as an old dray-horse about to be melted down for glue"; "It returns the theater . . . to the Thirties, a period the author seems never to have left." Brustein is explicit about what he conceives to be the shortcomings of *Incident*:

> Only one character has an option on the Truth, which the others will eventually take up with a cry of Eureka! . . . [Why should Von Berg] be held accountable for the politics of his relatives? . . . As for the ideas of the work . . . these have been hopelessly watered down. . . . It is apparently Mr. Miller's fate to stumble upon Pressing Questions long after more subtle minds have exhausted their possibilities, and then to pass them off as Profound Revelations—but all he adds are the capital

letters. The theme . . . is nothing but half-understood
Hannah Arendt . . . [who] showed how all of Europe
was implicated in the fate of the Jews, but she hardly exculpated the Germans. . . . Miller somehow manages to
get the Germans off the hook. If everybody is guilty,
then nobody is guilty, and the extermination of six
million can be attributed merely to the universality of
human evil, another agency recently discovered by the
author.

I have quoted Brustein at length because he expresses in a
summary fashion almost every possible negative critical reaction to the theme of the play; moreover, Brustein's view of
Miller has become the "official" one in some quarters. Whereas
Eric Bentley led the chorus of anti-Millerites in the Forties and
Fifties, criticizing Miller for writing exclusively of the "wholly
guilty and the wholly innocent," Brustein seems to have set the
tone for the Sixties, criticizing Miller now for writing exclusively of the "guilty." One thing, however, has remained
constant: Miller is still being damned as a "liberal" playwright.
    Miller is not an extreme relativist, not a thinker who holds
that *all* views are equally true . . . or equally absurd. Bayard
and Monceau are shining examples here. Although Miller permits them to express their thoughts and feelings in an open
fashion, he makes no pretense that their response to the cold
facts of the Nazi evil is an adequate or acceptable one. In his
review of *After the Fall*, Brustein accused Miller of political
ignorance; this charge cannot be leveled against *Incident*. Facts
do not support Bayard's Marxist arguments—the non-aggression
pact between Germany and Russia being one such fact (p. 30),
the working classes' refusal to destroy Fascism being another
(p. 34). Similarly, the approach advocated by Monceau in his
mentalist, or spiritualist, stance is untenable in the presence of
the Nazi furnace. The stage is "make believe"; but one cannot

"make believe" that the furnace is not the end—for Monceau goes into the office and he does not return.

When the critic comes to consider Von Berg and Leduc, however, the theme reveals itself in a more complex light. It is not correct to say that one character alone "has an option on the Truth." Leduc—and I take it that Brustein intends the doctor as Miller's sole custodian of "Truth"—is not without his ambiguities. In his argument with Monceau, Leduc criticizes the actor for his "desire to be sacrificed" (p. 48). Although the motivation differs in the case of Monceau's "sacrifice" and Von Berg's final gesture, the fact remains that essentially Von Berg's surrender of his pass to freedom is a "sacrifice." Metaphysically, it is a contradiction in terms to speak of "being" as "passive"; Von Berg's gesture is an *act*; but in the moral context of the play, or for that matter in the distinction that we make in the existential area of being, Von Berg's stance is the "passive," as opposed to the "active," way of combatting evil. Leduc does not understand "passivity" (p. 49). His posture is consistently "active." Recall his advice to the Major: "I'd believe it [that is, that you were no part of this evil] if you shot yourself. And better yet, if you took a few of them with you" (p. 53). Recall also his words to Von Berg which imply that even suicide is not "active" enough:

> if you had understood that Baron Kessler was in part . . . doing your will. You might have done something then, with your standing, and your name and your decency, aside from shooting yourself! (pp. 67-68)

That Von Berg's way is not the doctor's is made clear at the end of the play. When Von Berg presents Leduc with the pass to freedom, the latter "stares at him, a horrified look on his face"; "Leduc backs away, his hands springing to cover his eyes in the awareness of his own guilt"; "I wasn't asking you to do

this! You don't owe me this!"; but with his "eyes wide in awe
and terror," he nevertheless exits (p. 69). This is not the reaction of a man who has an "option on the Truth." One hesitates to repeat Pilate's question: "What is truth?" but perhaps
the point needs to be made that Von Berg's answer to the
dramatic question of the play would not seem to be entirely
acceptable, if acceptable at all, to all people. Douglas Watt,
for example, considers the play "philosophical claptrap"; Brustein is puzzled as to why Von Berg must die for Kessler's sins.
It is part of Miller's design, it appears, to stir the reader into
thinking about the issues involved. "What is truth?"—let the
reader place himself imaginatively in the position of the characters in *Incident at Vichy* and then ask himself the question.

The irony of the ending should also not be overlooked.
Leduc, the man who has preached responsibility for ninety-five
minutes, disappears with another's pass to freedom. Leduc, who
knows the secrets of the human heart, stands in "awe and
terror" in the presence of one who knows "so little about people," but who has learned enough about himself, and other
men, now—thanks to the good doctor—to offer himself as an
oblation for the sins of mankind. Would Leduc, in Von Berg's
circumstances, have practiced what he has preached? The answer is far from simple. Miller has come a long distance from
the "straightforward" thesis drama of *All My Sons*.

Nor is this the end of Leduc's complexity in relation to the
theme. There is the loss of his ideals when faced by death
(p. 63), a loss which Von Berg seeks to recover through his
death. Who has an "option on the Truth" here? There is also
Leduc's dispute with the Major. When Leduc gives the Major
his advice (quoted above, p. 53), the latter asks: "Why do you
deserve to live more than I do?" and Leduc replies: "Because
I am incapable of doing what you are doing. I am better for
the world than you" (p. 54). The Major proceeds to examine
Leduc's moral superiority:

Major: If you were released, and the others were kept . . . would you refuse?

. . . .

Leduc: No.

Major: And walk out of that door with a light heart?

Leduc—*he is looking at the floor now:* I don't know. *He starts to put his trembling hands into his pockets.*

Major: Don't hide your hands. I am trying to understand why you are better for the world than me. Why do you hide your hands? Would you go out that door with a light heart . . . ? Why are you better than anybody else?

Leduc: I have no duty to make a gift of myself to your sadism.

Major: But I do? To others' sadism? Of myself? I have that duty and you do not? To make a gift of myself?

Leduc—*looks at the Professor and the Police Captain, glances back at the Major:* I have nothing to say.

Major: That's better. (pp. 56-57)

Who has an "option on the Truth" here? It will be recalled that shortly before this discussion, Leduc had temporarily refused to escape with the boy and Lebeau because he was reluctant to be "slaughtered" (p. 48)—that is, he did not want to make, at least no sooner than necessary, a "gift" of himself. That he finally does decide to make a dash for freedom seems more an act born of desperation, since he is faced with death anyway, than genuine courage, the kind of courage that Von Berg evinces. It should also be noted, finally, that the dialogue quoted above is a good example of how Miller combines "drama" and "ideas" into "drama of ideas."

How adequate are those "ideas"? *Incident at Vichy*, like *The Crucible*, is a philosophical melodrama. In *The Playwright as Thinker*, Eric Bentley has used this term to describe the plays of Sartre (see, for example, *The Flies*) as a "combination of histrionics and serious thought," and with no "slur" in mind. Shaw has also exploited this kind of theater. But critics have not always applauded Shaw, Sartre, and Miller in their efforts here; the usual charge is that the plays deal with symbols instead of "people" and that there is too much "talk" and too little "action." The three words with quotes embracing them should suggest that some redefinitions of terms are in order. I have tried to show that in *Incident at Vichy* there is both talk and action (the duplication, or redundancy, of *After the Fall* is of course not intended here), and that at times the talk *is* the action. I have also argued that Von Berg and Leduc are more than mere symbols, that question marks surround their behavior, particularly that of Leduc. True, the other characters, representing for the most part but a single idea, are relatively flat. From that standpoint, the play seems simple. But *Incident*, like *Crucible*, is only apparently a realistic play. Compare these two works, for example, with a genuine realistic piece, *All My Sons*. In the early play, an attempt was made to make *each* of the characters complex combinations of good and bad, whereas in the philosophical melodramas the tendency is to account for moral complexity by the *range* of characters represented—that is, *all* the characters *together* comprise the necessary thematic complexity. Looked at from one angle, then, *Incident* indeed appears simple; looked at from another perspective, however, the play seems complex.

Whether it is Miller—or Brustein—who fails to understand Miss Arendt's *Eichmann in Jerusalem* or whether neither of them misunderstands that book, is irrelevant here. ("It seemed to me," says Miller in *Life*, February 7, 1964, "that she was trying to make a spectacularly simple and quite evident point. Namely, that the significant truth about Eichmann was not that he was a monster but that, in order to exercise his monstrousness . . . he had to have the moral permission of others . . . even to Jews and to well-meaning Gentiles who . . . were less than total in their active opposition to barbarity. But the suggestion that 'we' could . . . hear responsibility for what 'we' abhor was turned upside down by some people so that Miss Arendt was made to seem an apologist for Eichmann.") Not irrelevant, though, is the fact that Brustein seems to miss the thrust of Miller's play. Miller has not, any more than Miss Arendt, "exculpated the Germans." The dramatic image of the play makes the Nazi evil enormously vivid. What Miller has done is to extend the limits of guilt beyond the narrowly juridical until complicity shades over into active moral permissiveness and passive acceptance of evil. Miller has written a play, not a legal brief. In *After the Fall,* complicity seemed strained and remote; in *Incident at Vichy* it is rendered concrete and immediate. Admittedly, there are times when the dialogue becomes too abstract; but on the whole the language tends to spring naturally from character and incident. It is also true that *Incident,* like *Crucible,* lacks that sensuous quality found in *Salesman* and *A View;* this is an inherent limitation perhaps of *philosophical* melodrama, and for that reason might not be for all tastes. For that matter, *melodrama* has never been for all tastes. And it is not difficult to find the melodrama in *Vichy.* The repeated appearances of the police guard who silently regards the prisoners, early in the play, is an obvious instance. (Within the context of the play, however, this device is less crude than analysis might suggest.) Most of the characters, it might also be objected, are—and this is usually the case in melodrama—finished when they make their first appearance; they do not, save for Leduc and Von Berg, take shape before us. Even the ending, limited as it is to a gesture, has, some might argue, melodramatic overtones. Brevity sets certain limits on depth, and the structure, almost flawless by conventional standards, is perhaps too neat for some readers. There is some truth in these observations, and no balanced critique of *Incident at Vichy* should ignore them. In my opinion, however, the credits outweigh the debits in a final accounting of the play and Miller's use of the detention room in Vichy as a symbol of man's indifference to his fellows in *any* human situation is a valid and compelling one.

Finally, Von Berg is "held accountable for the politics" of his cousin because the Prince shut his eyes to his relative's anti-Semitism and murder. Would the Nazis have succeeded without the complicity of others? The question is not academic. Von Berg's complicity is made plain. But nobody in the play, except Leduc—who does *not* have an "option on the Truth"—says that we are *all* responsible; the reader infers as much from the action, and either accepts or rejects the idea according to his lights. Which is another reason why *Incident At Vichy* is not to be confused with a thesis play. As I have stressed, the play represents a complex range of possible alternatives to evil. For some, and Brustein is not alone here, these important questions have been "exhausted" by minds more profound than Miller's; for others, the last word has "not yet been spoken." In his review of *The Holocaust Kingdom*, Edward T. Gargan says: "How frustrating that the unmeasurable crimes and the suffering of the victims must submit to the limits and possibilities of art or be forgotten. Unless art keeps their memory, the tears and the trembling of all the children who walked to the terrible school of the gas chamber will be no part of our lives. . . . The words that will console them have not yet been spoken."

It might very well be an exaggeration to say, with Taubman, that Miller's play "returns the theater to greatness," but one might not hesitate to agree when that same critic affirms that *Incident at Vichy* is "a moving play, a searching play, one of the most important plays of our time."

CONCLUSION

" There is, then, no smooth line of development in Miller's work; no elegant pattern of growth from crude experimental efforts to finished master works. True, *All My Sons* is defective; but *A Memory of Two Mondays* follows *The Crucible* and *A View from the Bridge*, playing on the same bill with *A Memory*, precedes *After the Fall*. Even Miller's best plays are, if not vastly, at least manifestly unequal in merit. Compare, for example, *Death of a Salesman* with *Incident at Vichy*. Structurally, Miller's best plays—*Death of a Salesman* and *A View from the Bridge*—are complex and coherent. If *The Crucible* and *Incident at Vichy* are in danger of being too "neat," they are saved from being "empty" by their density of theme. *All My Sons* fails, however, because it is both neat *and* empty. There is nothing neat, though, about *A Memory of Two Mondays* and *After the Fall*, for these plays are awkward and episodic. Miller, it would seem, is no Chekhov—he needs a plot.

The stock criticism of Miller's characters is that they are too often schematized, too nearly black and white puppets. This charge, as my analysis of the plays suggests, needs to be drastically qualified. Willy Loman, Biff Loman, Eddie Carbone, Rodolpho, even Leduc are all complex creations. Even in *A Memory of Two Mondays*, Miller manages to partially redeem that play through his robust portrayals of Gus and Kenneth. Every playwright produces flat and static characters, and Miller has produced his share of them. At times, this appears to be a fault—one thinks at once of Linda and Happy in *Death of a Salesman*; but no sane critic evaluates a play solely on char-

179

acter, much less on the evidence of merely one or two unsatisfy-
ing characters in an otherwise excellent work. It might be
objected that *The Crucible* and *Incident at Vichy* are too neat
and schematized in characterization, but I have attempted to
meet this criticism in my treatment of these plays by arguing
for their full range of representation and their thematic density.
Clearly Von Berg and Leduc are more complex and ambiguous
creations than Joe and Chris Keller in *All My Sons*.

Thematically, and this is one measure of his achievement,
Miller has created a related body of work. Certain themes,
such as "integrity" or "compromise," may be—and too often
are—isolated for discussion; but this abstraction, perfectly valid
on one level, tends to ignore other themes in Miller's work,
themes which I have analyzed in my studies of individual plays.
And these themes are not easily given one-word tags. To say,
for instance, that Willy Loman, John Proctor, and Eddie Carbone are all concerned with their "integrity" is true—but that
observation scarcely does justice to the thematic complexity of
their respective plays. It may seem that I am undercutting my
previous assertion that Miller's plays are related. What I am
trying to say, however, is that there is both unity and diversity
in Miller's work, and that we oversimplify and distort his
achievement by focusing too narrowly and too insistently on one
or two obvious and fashionable aspects of his work. One must
beware, for example, of branding Miller merely a "social"
dramatist, for as analysis of the plays makes clear he is equally
a "psychological" playwright. At his best, Miller has avoided
the extremes of clinical psychiatric case studies on the one hand
and mere sociological reports on the other. Assimilating avail-
able technical devices to his own unique aims, he has indicated,
often in the face of incredible critical stupidity, contradiction,
and malice, how the dramatist might maintain in delicate balance both personal and social motivation. Not all modern playwrights, it need scarcely be added, have succeeded in projecting
such integral motivation. Nor is it correct to say that the main

burden of guilt in his plays is borne by society. Miller's characters—Willy Loman, John Proctor, Eddie Carbone, Quentin,
and Von Berg—"take their life in their arms" (as Holga puts
it in *After the Fall*), with the result that the accusing finger of
guilt is leveled at *both* the individual *and* society. If one rejects
Miller because he is too "narrow," because he lacks a meta-
physic or a theology of crisis, then one should be prepared, I
think, to reject some of the most vital playwrights of the
modern theater.

Finally, an alert and sympathetic reader will not blur the
distinction between a thesis drama like *All My Sons* and a play
like *The Crucible*, or between *All My Sons* and *Incident at
Vichy*. In *All My Sons*, character is made to jump in order to
drive home the message and structure is a series of gross im-
probabilities. *The Crucible*, however, is another matter, for
neither character nor structure is violated to make a point.
John Proctor's death "proves" nothing, because the reader is
given an option on how to interpret the "meaning" of his
death; Danforth, for example, does not put a bullet through his
head when John strides to his death; nor is there anything incredible about John's willingness to die—there is, in short,
smooth transition here, not a jump. Moreover, in *All My Sons*
the full range of human responses to events is not always in
evidence; for instance Chris and the other soldiers are idealized,
while Joe and others on the home front are made to regard the
war as, according to Chris, merely a "bus accident." *The
Crucible* and *Incident at Vichy* avoid this oversimplification
through the use of multiple character viewpoints on the action.
It is not easy to classify plays like *The Crucible* or *Incident at
Vichy*—they might be called "morality plays" or "philosophical
melodramas"—but however classified they should not be confused with thesis drama. Even Miller's most ardent supporters
have recognized his *tendency* toward the didactic, a tendency
that is the root cause of the previously noted criticisms of his
"neat structures" and "schematized characterizations," but it

cannot be too strongly emphasized that in his *best* work—*Death of a Salesman, The Crucible, A View from the Bridge,* and *Incident at Vichy*—he has transcended, at times in spite of his "intentions," the defects that distinguish *All My Sons* and *After the Fall.*

In *Incident at Vichy,* Miller reveals that he still has much to say and the formal discipline to say it effectively. One would appear to be justified, therefore, in anticipating other important, perhaps even more significant, plays from Arthur Miller.

BIBLIOGRAPHY

CHAPTER ONE: *All My Sons*

William Archer, *Play-Making* (New York, 1960); Arthur Boggs, "*Oedipus* and *All My Sons*," *Personalist*, XLII (October 1961), 555-560; Harold Clurman, *Lies Like Truth* (New York, 1958); Arthur Ganz, "The Silence of Arthur Miller," *Drama Survey*, III (October 1963), 224-237; Robert Hogan, *Arthur Miller* (Minneapolis, 1964); Joseph Wood Krutch, "Drama," *Nation*, CLXIV (February 15, 1947), 191, 193; John Howard Lawson, *Theory and Technique of Playwriting* (New York, 1960); Max Lerner, *Actions and Passions* (New York, 1949); Leonard Moss, "Arthur Miller and the Common Man's Language," *Modern Drama*, VII (May 1964), 52-59; Kappo Phelan, "The Stage and Screen," *Commonweal*, XLV (February 14, 1947), 445-446; Dennis Welland, *Arthur Miller* (London, 1961); Arvin R. Wells, "The Living and the Dead in *All My Sons*," *Modern Drama*, VII (May 1964), 46-51; Samuel A. Yorks, "Joe Keller and His Sons," *Western Humanities Review*, XIII (Autumn 1959), 401-407.

CHAPTER TWO: *Death of a Salesman*

Eric Bentley, "Theater," New Republic, CXXXIII (December, 1955), 21-22 and *In Search of Theater* (New York, 1954); Sister M. Bettina, "Willy Loman's Brother Ben: Tragic Insight in *Death of a Salesman*," *Modern Drama*, IV (February 1962), 409-412; Judah Bierman, and others, *The Dramatic Experience* (Englewood Cliffs, N. J., 1958); Clurman; Alan S. Downer, *Fifty Years of American Drama, 1900-1950* (Chicago, 1951); Tom F. Driver, "Strength and Weakness in Arthur Miller," *Tulane Drama Review*, IV (May 1960), 48-52; Richard J. Foster, "Confusion and Tragedy: The Failure of Miller's *Salesman*," in *Two Modern*

American Tragedies, ed. John D. Hurrell (New York, 1961); A. Howard Fuller, "A Salesman is Everybody," *Fortune*, XXXIX (May 1949), 79-80; Ganz; Bamber Gascoigne, *Twentieth-Century Drama* (London, 1962); John Gassner, "Tragic Perspectives," *Tulane Drama Review*, II (May 1958), 7-22, and *The Theater in Our Times* (New York, 1954) and *Theater At the Crossroads* (New York, 1960); John A. Hagopian, "Arthur Miller: The *Salesman's* Two Cases," *Modern Drama*, VI (September 1963), 117-125; Joseph A. Hynes, "Attention Must Be Paid . . ." *College English*, XXIII (April 1962), 574-578; Laurence Kitchin, *Mid-Century Drama* (London, 1960); Joseph Wood Krutch, "Drama," *Nation*, CLXVIII (March 5, 1949), 283- 284; John Mander, *The Writer and Commitment* (Philadelphia, 1962); G. Emile McAnany, "The Tragic Commitment," *Modern Drama*, V (May 1962), 11-20; William G. McCollum, *Tragedy* (New York, 1957); C. Wright Mills, *White Collar* (New York, 1951); Herbert J. Muller, *The Spirit of Tragedy* (New York, 1956); George Jean Nathan, *The Magic Mirror* (New York, 1960); Elder Olson, *Tragedy and the Theory of Drama* (Detroit, 1961); Daniel E. Schneider, *The Psychoanalyst and the Artist* (New York 1962); Robert Boies Sharpe, *Irony in the Drama* (Chapel Hill, 1959); Paul N. Siegal, "Willy Loman and King Lear," *College English*, XVII (March 1956), 341-345; Gerald Weales, "Arthur Miller: Man and His Image," *Tulane Drama Review*, VII (Fall 1962), 165-180; Dennis Welland, *Arthur Miller* (London, 1961); T. C. Worsley, "Poetry Without Words," *New Statesman and Nation*, XXXVIII (August 6, 1949), 146-147.

CHAPTER THREE: *The Crucible*

Eric Bentley, "Miller's Innocence," *New Republic*, CXXVIII (February 16, 1953), 22-23; John Mason Brown, "Seeing Things," *Saturday Review of Literature*, XXXVI (February 14, 1953), 41-42; Alan S. Downer, *Recent American Drama* (Minneapolis, 1961); Lajos Egri, *The Art of Dramatic Writing* (New York, 1946); Gascoigne; Gassner, *Theater at the Crossroads*; Walter Kerr, *How Not to Write a Play* (New York, 1955); Freda Kirchwey, "*The Crucible*," *Nation*, CLXXVI (February 7, 1953), 131-132; Lawson; David Levine, "Salem Witchcraft in Recent Fiction and Drama," *New England Quarterly*, XXVIII (December 1955), 537-546; Olson; Henry Popkin, "Arthur Miller's *The Crucible*," *College*

English, XXVI (November 1964), 139-146; D. D. Raphael, *The Paradox of Tragedy* (Bloomington, 1960); Sharpe; Kenneth Tynan, *Curtains* (New York, 1961); Robert Warshow, "The Liberal Conscience in *The Crucible*," *Commentary*, XV (March 1953), 265-271; Richard Watts, Jr., "Introduction" to *The Crucible* (New York, 1959); Weales; Welland.

CHAPTER FOUR: *A Memory of Two Mondays*

Gascoigne; Walcott Gibbs, "The Theater," *New Yorker*, XXI (October 8, 1955), 92, 94-95; Richard Hayes, "The Stage," *Commonweal*, LXIII (November 4, 1955), 117-118; Hogan; Mills; Moss; Welland; Raymond Williams, "The Realism of Arthur Miller," *Critical Quarterly*, I (Summer 1959), 140-149.

CHAPTER FIVE: *A View from the Bridge*

Richard Barksdale, "Social Background in the Plays of Miller and Williams," *CLA Journal*, VI (March 1963), 161-169; Bentley, *New Republic* (1955); Edmund Bergler, *The Basic Neurosis* (New York, 1949); Downer, *Recent American Drama*; Richard A. Duprey, "Arthur Miller," *Catholic World*, CXCIII (September 1961), 394-395; Richard Findlater, "No Time for Tragedy?," *Twentieth Century*, CLXI (January 1957), 56-62; Ganz; Gascoigne; Gassner, *Theater At the Crossroads*; Anthony Hartley, "Waterfront," *Spectator*, CXCVII (October 19, 1956), 538-540; Hayes; Henry Hewes, "Broadway Postscript," *Saturday Review of Literature*, XXXVIII (October 15, 1955), 25-26; Hogan; Lawson; Moss; Sharpe; Gerald Weales, "Plays and Analysis," *Commonweal*, LXVI (July 12, 1957), 382-383; Welland; Williams; T. C. Worsley, "Realistic Melodrama," *New Statesman and Nation*, LII (October 20, 1956), 482; Euphemia V. R. Wyatt, "Theater," *Catholic World*, CLXXXII (November 1955), 144-145.

CHAPTER SIX: *After the Fall*

Robert Brustein, "Arthur Miller's Mea Culpa," *New Republic*, CL (February 8, 1964), 26-28, 30; Francis Fergusson, *The Idea of a Theater* (New York, 1949); Arthur Ganz, "Arthur Miller: After the Silence," *Drama Survey*, III (Fall 1964), 520-530; Richard Gilman, "The Stage," *Commonweal*, LXXIX (February 14, 1964), 600-601 and *Book Week* (March 8, 1964), 6, 13; Hogan; Carl Jung, *The Undiscovered Self* (New York, 1959); John R. Milton, "The Esthetic Fault of Strindberg's 'Dream Plays'," *Tulane Drama Review*, IV (March 1960), 108-116; Tom Prideaux, *Life*, LVI (February 7, 1964), 64B-64D; Gordon Rogoff, "Theater," *Nation*, CXCVIII (February 10, 1964), 153-154; Albert Schweitzer, *Civilization and Ethics* (London, 1946); Weales, *Tulane*.

CHAPTER SEVEN: *Incident at Vichy*

Eric Bentley, *The Playwright as Thinker* (New York, 1955); Robert Brustein, "Muddy Track At Lincoln Center," *New Republic*, CL (December 26, 1964), 26-27; Edward T. Gargan, "Reflections on Tunneling Out of an Antheap," [rev. of *The Holocaust Kingdom*], *Commonweal*, LXXXI (February 12, 1965), 644; Henry Hewes, "Broadway Postscript," *Saturday Review of Literature*, XLVII (December 19, 1964), 24; Howard Taubman, *New York Times* (December 4, 1964), sec. L, 44; Douglas Watt, *New York Daily News* (December 4, 1964), 64.